## Awards and praise for the original edition:

Parent Council Selection

National Parenting Publications
(NAPPA) "Parenting Resources Award"

Parents' Choice Recommended

*Read, America!* Selection

"Practical . . . kid-friendly." **—Youthworker**

"Filled with information and advice to help ease the transition from childhood to adolescence." **—Booklist**

"*Too Old for This, Too Young for That!* is full of straight talk, tips, and advice." **—Girls' Life**

"An informative and delightful guide through these turbulent days." **—Voice of Youth Advocates**

# Too Old for This,

# Too Young for That!

## Your Survival Guide for the Middle School Years

Harriet S. Mosatche, Ph.D.
Karen Unger, M.A.

free spirit
PUBLISHING®

**Library of Congress Cataloging-in-Publication Data**
Mosatche, Harriet S., 1949–
  Too old for this, too young for that! : your survival guide for the middle school years / Harriet S. Mosatche and Karen Unger. — Updated 2nd ed.
    p. cm.
  Includes index.
  ISBN 978-1-57542-352-4
  1. Preteens—Life skills guides—Juvenile literature. 2. Preteens—Psychology—Juvenile literature. 3. Middle school students—Life skills guides—Juvenile literature. 4. Middle school students—Psychology—Juvenile literature. 5. Teenagers—Life skills guides—Juvenile literature. 6. Adolescent psychology—Juvenile literature.  I. Unger, Karen, 1954– II. Title.
  HQ777.15.M67 2010
  646.700835—dc22

                                                                                    2010014588

Free Spirit Publishing does not have control over or assume responsibility for author or third-party websites and their content. At the time of this book's publication, all facts and figures cited within are the most current available. All telephone numbers, addresses, and website URLs are accurate and active; all publications, organizations, websites, and other resources exist as described in this book; and all have been verified as of May 2010. If you find an error or believe that a resource listed here is not as described, please contact Free Spirit Publishing. Parents, teachers, and other adults: We strongly urge you to monitor children's use of the Internet.

Reading Level Grades 6 & Up; Interest Level Ages 10–14;
Fountas & Pinnell Guided Reading Level X

Cover and interior design by Michelle Lee
Illustrations by Jimmy Holder

10 9 8 7 6 5 4 3 2 1
Printed in the United States of America
U19810710

**Free Spirit Publishing Inc.**
217 Fifth Avenue North, Suite 200
Minneapolis, MN 55401-1299
(612) 338-2068
help4kids@freespirit.com
www.freespirit.com

# Dedication

To my children—Rob and Liz—who survived the middle school, high school, and college years with experiences that continue to inform my writing, and who inspire me every day. **—H.S.M.**

To my son who first inspired the idea for a book for boys and girls—a book that has remained popular and helpful to many middle school kids—and who now, as a middle school kid himself, has helped keep the book relevant. I am grateful for him every day. **—K.U.**

# Acknowledgments

We would especially like to acknowledge all of the middle school kids with whom we spoke and whose quotes appear throughout the book. A special shout-out to George O. and Allan R. for all their help. Thank you so much for your honesty and insights. We also would like to thank Free Spirit Publishing and its founder and publisher Judy Galbraith for offering kids a wealth of books that enlighten families and help kids grow up in not-so-easy times. Our editor Douglas Fehlen was a true joy to work with, and we appreciate his many helpful suggestions. And we would like to thank our families—our husbands, who supported us as we were immersed in writing and revising, and our parents, who were our guides to surviving not just the teen years, but also the challenges and adventures we have met throughout our lives.

# Contents

## Survival Tip #5
## Find, Make, and Keep Friends................................84

## Survival Tip #6
## Make the Most of Middle School.......................114

# Survival Tip #7
## Take Charge of Your Life .................................142

# Introduction

Have you noticed that your life seems to be getting more complicated? Maybe you feel confused or worried one moment, then thrilled or excited the next. It might even seem like you're on an enormous roller coaster. You may not be sure how you got on or how to get off, but you know there's no turning back now.

Welcome to the middle school years! Like a roller coaster ride, this time in your life has ups, downs, twists, turns, and sudden starts and stops. Sometimes you may wonder how you can possibly hang on . . . but at least you're not on the ride alone.

Why is middle school so different from elementary school? Because practically everything has changed. Not only do you have more teachers, subjects, homework, projects, and tests, but you might also have a homeroom, a locker, more clubs and activities, and other new things to handle. Your friends and classmates probably don't look, act, or dress the way they used to. What you talk about together may be different, too. Everyone might now seem a lot more concerned about who's coolest, cutest, or most popular.

Life at home may also be changing. Parents* might suddenly make more rules and give you additional chores. Maybe you feel like adults at home often treat you like a kid, even as they say they want you to act more grown up. You're not a child anymore, but you're not grown-up either. You're in between, and sometimes that's a hard place to be.

If you're between the ages of ten and fourteen, changes are happening to you inside and out. You probably don't think, feel, look, or act like you used to. During these years, you might:

- grow about two to five inches and gain around five to fifteen pounds per year (which is completely normal but can feel totally weird)

> "During my first day of middle school, I couldn't even find the boys' bathroom, let alone my locker and all my classes. But in a day or two, I started to adjust."
> **—Tim, 14**

> "I was so happy to start middle school. It's exciting. I have more freedom and more fun."
> **—Christina, 11**

> "Middle school is about changing a lot—friends, school, even me. I grew four inches this year!"
> **—Carlos, 13**

*This book often uses the word *parents,* but the information in it can be helpful whether you live with one or two parents, another adult relative, a stepfamily, a foster family, or other people. When you see the word *parents,* you can think of the adults who are responsible for you.

- mature more quickly or slowly than other kids (which is normal, too)
- notice pimples erupting on your face, hair where there was no hair before, and other embarrassing things
- feel excited yet scared about puberty and all the changes that come with it
- worry a lot about making friends, having enough friends, being popular, or finding a boyfriend or girlfriend
- be lost, bored, confused, or frustrated in school
- feel sure that no one on earth understands you

With so much happening all at once, who wouldn't feel a little overwhelmed?

The middle school years are unpredictable, but they're also exciting and filled with possibility. You can use this time to:

- explore your talents
- strengthen your skills at school and in athletics and other activities
- learn to understand and deal with your emotions
- build lasting friendships
- form better relationships with the people in your family
- set goals and find ways to reach them
- make plans for your future

The middle school years are a time when you're figuring out who you are and who you want to be. (This is a lifelong process, by the way, so don't worry if you don't figure it all out.) You'll become more of an individual, with your own point of view, and you'll start to find new ways to express yourself—through your activities, schoolwork, clothes, and hobbies. You're also old enough to decide how to spend some of your own money, go more places with friends (without your parents), and choose which activities to pursue. You get to do more and be more, and this is the fun part of the middle school years.

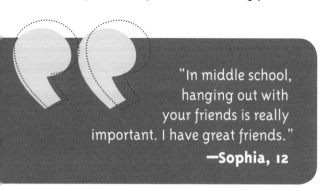

"In middle school, hanging out with your friends is really important. I have great friends."
**—Sophia, 12**

Middle school can be a really terrific time in your life, but it has its rough moments, too. We wrote *Too Old for This, Too Young for That!* to help tweens and teens overcome these challenges and make the middle school years the best they can be. The book is organized around seven Survival Tips that cover every part of your life: family, friends, feelings, body changes, school, and making choices. Up-to-date information answers questions you might have about getting older. You'll also find quotes from real middle school students, quizzes to explore interests, advice for tough times, and fun activities you can use to take charge of your life.

Maybe you're wondering what two adults like us could possibly know about middle school. The answer: plenty. We survived it, just like you will, and we remember what it was like. We know how it feels to be too shy to raise your hand in class, even though you definitely know the answer. Or to be embarrassed beyond belief if your parents pick you up at school and don't wait in the car like you asked them to. We know about getting glasses or braces just when you least want them. Or having a crush on someone who doesn't even know you're alive.

Our entire careers have involved helping tweens and teens handle the changes that come with getting older. Over the years, students have shared with us their experiences, feelings, problems, mistakes, successes, and dreams. This book brings together what we have learned, and now we hope it helps *you* navigate the challenges of middle school.

Feel free to contact us with questions or comments. You can write to us at this address:

**Harriet S. Mosatche**
**Karen Unger**
c/o Free Spirit Publishing Inc.
217 Fifth Avenue North, Suite 200
Minneapolis, MN 55401-1299

Or email us at: help4kids@freespirit.com

**P.S.** A thirteen-year-old we know once said that life as a middle school student is fun because you have "more freedom, privileges, and responsibilities." We couldn't agree more that life during these years can be great. There's a lot to look forward to, so enjoy the ride!

# Get Used to Your Changing Body

A lot of the changes that occur during the middle school years are related to puberty. When your body begins the passage into adulthood, it can be exciting but also confusing. Before you start seeing physical changes on the outside, your body starts to change on the inside. Your brain and certain glands begin to release larger amounts of hormones (powerful chemical substances) into your bloodstream. These hormones play an important role in your body's development.

Puberty isn't a single event or something that happens overnight. It's a process that lasts for several years. That's why it's a good idea to get used to your changing body. **Survival Tip #1** can help you do that.

# You're Changing Inside and Out

When you start puberty, your body begins to grow very fast. The only time your body grows *more quickly* is in the first year of life. Back then, your brain and body were developing rapidly, and the same is true now. Your appetite might increase, as well as your need for sleep. That's because your growing body requires a lot of rest and nutrients to support all the physical changes it's going through.

When puberty begins, you may notice that the jacket sleeve that used to reach below your wrist is now above it. The jeans' legs you once tripped over might now only go to your ankles. It can seem like your entire wardrobe is shrinking, but what you're experiencing is known as a growth spurt. Your feet might grow by as much as a shoe size each month. Or your hands may quickly get larger so you can grasp a basketball with greater ease. The middle school years are filled with these kinds of surprises.

What can be even more unpredictable is *when* body changes occur. You may start changing earlier or later than your friends. And these changes might happen more quickly or slowly than they do

"I hate that kids in school laugh when my voice cracks."
—**Alex, 11**

"My legs are getting really hairy and it's embarrassing."
—**Sarah, 12**

"They have these thin walls in the gym, and us girls can hear boys talk about how big certain private body parts are. Some girls compare chest size, too."
—**Amelia, 12**

"I'm glad I finally started growing. I used to be shortest in my class."
—**Latrell, 13**

for others. There's no need to worry. You'll develop at a pace that's right for you.

## Changes in Boys

Boys start going through puberty anywhere from about ages ten to fifteen. The first sign is usually a major growth spurt. Another thing a guy will notice is his voice deepening. Boys often welcome this change because they sound more masculine for the first time. Voice changes—like other puberty developments—don't occur all at once. Instead, changes in the voice take place gradually and may involve squeaking and croaking.

"It's hard to get used to all of the changes my body is going through, but it feels good to know that I am getting closer to being a man."

—Chen, 13

Other changes for boys during puberty include:

- the appearance of underarm and facial hair
- an increase in body hair
- the lengthening and widening of the penis
- enlargement of the testes
- growth of pubic hair (it gradually becomes darker and curlier)
- more frequent erections (meaning the penis fills with blood and becomes hard)
- the first ejaculation (release of semen, the fluid containing sperm)
- nocturnal emissions (or "wet dreams"), meaning ejaculation during sleep

All of these changes are normal, and they take place gradually. They also occur at a different pace for every boy. Guys who are worried about body changes (or the pace at which they occur) can talk to

*The Guy Book: An Owner's Manual* by Mavis Jukes. Get the scoop on puberty and other subjects (like feelings and relationships) in this engaging book for guys.

*The What's Happening to My Body? Book for Boys* by Lynda Madaras with Area Madaras. This resource has information on body changes, sexuality, zits, facial hair, body odor, and many other topics.

a parent or another trusted person who is older. Getting the perspective of someone who has been in the same situation can be a big help.

## Changes in Girls

Generally, girls start to mature anywhere from ages eight to fifteen. It's often a couple of years before boys. One of the first signs of puberty is the budding of a girl's breasts. This starts with just a little swelling under the nipples. Breasts come in a wide variety of sizes and shapes, just like penises do. Sometimes one breast may develop more quickly than the other, which is nothing to worry about. Breasts usually even out, but it's unlikely for them to ever look exactly alike.

Many girls may start wearing a bra for the first time during the middle school years. Bra shopping can make any girl nervous at first. But a talk with her mom, an older sister, or a cousin can help. And knowledgeable salespeople know just how to find the right size bra.

Soon after their breasts begin to develop, girls start to grow taller and at a faster rate. The body develops more curves,

"My aunt took me shopping for my first bra. I probably would have been a lot more nervous without her help."
—**Shanice, 13**

with some weight gain in the hips, buttocks, and thighs. While some girls may see the weight gain as "getting fat," the body is simply taking on a new shape. This is perfectly normal.

Other changes for girls during puberty include:

- the appearance of underarm hair
- the darkening and increasing of arm and leg hair
- growth of pubic hair (it gradually becomes darker and curlier)
- an increase in discharge from the vagina

One of the biggest changes girls undergo is *menarche*. This is the onset of menstruation, or the first period. Usually, menarche occurs about one and a half to two years after a girl's breasts begin to grow.

During the menstrual cycle, one of the ovaries (there are two of them) releases an ovum, or egg. It travels through one of the fallopian tubes (there are two of those as well) to reach the uterus. While the egg travels, the lining of the uterus thickens and fills with extra blood and tissue to prepare for possible fertilization by a sperm. If the egg isn't fertilized, the blood-filled tissue comes apart and passes out of the girl's body through her vagina.

Many girls are afraid that the blood will gush out, maybe during school, and everyone will see it. However, first periods are typically light, and the blood looks like a brownish stain or just a few drops of red blood. In the beginning, periods may not occur once a month, which is normal. Once periods become more regular, they occur monthly and last anywhere from three to seven days. The first days are the heaviest, with the blood flow gradually decreasing. Girls can use tampons or sanitary pads to absorb the blood.

"I just started my period, and I'm feeling really stressed about it. I'm afraid everyone will know. I guess this is what it means to get older."

**—Carly, 12**

When girls have their period, they can do anything they'd normally do: go to school, play sports, swim, shower, take a bath, or whatever. Some girls feel tired or irritable before or during their period, and this is natural. Many girls experience cramps, which are actually muscle contractions of the uterus. Exercise often helps, and so does getting a bit more rest. If discomfort is severe, a doctor might recommend a pain-relief medication.

Girls are likely to feel a mix of emotions when they get their periods the first time. It's normal to feel scared, happy, confused, proud, grown-up, worried, or even a little bit sad, because it signals leaving a stage of life. Girls often find that talking to someone—a mom, a coach, or a school nurse—about their feelings and questions can help. Books and websites about puberty can also be helpful.

**CHECK IT OUT**

*The Care and Keeping of You: The Body Book for Girls* by Valorie Schaefer. Look here for straightforward information on body changes and what to expect during puberty.

*The What's Happening to My Body? Book for Girls* by Lynda Madaras with Area Madaras. This book features helpful information on physical development, menstruation, emotions, sexuality, and many other topics.

# Coping with Changes

Whether you're a boy or a girl, and no matter where you live, you have something in common with everyone else your age: body changes. When you look at the others in your grade, you'll see that some of the girls tower over the boys, while other girls are smaller. Some girls may have their period or may be wearing a bra, while others haven't developed breasts yet. Some guys may be growing a mustache, while others don't have a hint of facial hair. Some may already have a deep voice, while others haven't experienced voice changes yet. The important thing to remember is that everyone changes at his or her own pace.

No matter who you are or what stage you're at, change can feel strange. It may help to write about changes and how you feel about them. You can write in a journal or note-book, or you might write on a computer. Record the date, what about you has changed, what you like about the change, and what you don't like about it. You don't have to limit your writing to body changes. Instead, write about other things that might be on your mind—how you feel, what happened at school on a particular day, your likes and dislikes, or what dreams and goals you have.

> "If you're going through puberty at a different rate than your friends, you might feel uncomfortable about what's happening. You may feel too small or too big or too gangly. It can help to remember that everyone has to go through different stages."
>
> **—Sam, 14**

Even after writing about the changes you're going through, you may still have questions about them. Maybe you doubt whether you're developing in a normal way. If you have concerns, talk to a parent or another older person you trust about what you're going through.

**CHECK IT OUT**

**TeensHealth**
**www.teenshealth.org**
Visit this website for helpful info and advice on body changes, sexuality, and other topics related to puberty.

**We Are Talking Teen Health**
**www.pamf.org/teen**
This site, developed by doctors, educators, and teens, features information on puberty and other important health topics.

# Give Your Body the Fuel It Needs

During the middle school years, you're starting to make more decisions about food. Maybe you fix your own breakfast, eat a school lunch, make yourself a snack when you get home, and even prepare dinner some nights. You probably have a little more spending money, too, so you might buy food at the mall or other places where you hang out. How well you eat and treat your body is often totally up to you.

You're growing so rapidly that you're probably not surprised to find you need some extra nutrients during the middle school years. Greater amounts of protein, for example, are required at your age compared to what you needed as a child. Proteins help supply energy and keep your body tissues healthy. You can get the extra protein you need from meat, poultry, fish, milk, and nuts.

Calcium supports your growing bone structure, so you need even more of this mineral now than when you're an adult. It's important to consume a lot of milk and other dairy products to get added calcium each day. You'll also find this mineral in broccoli, almonds, and calcium-fortified orange juice.

Another mineral you need is iron. Girls require fifty percent more iron from the time they start puberty until well into adulthood. This is because iron is lost in the menstrual blood flow. Boys need extra iron, too, because during the middle school years, their blood volume and tissue growth increases. Red meat, peanut butter, apricots, and dark, leafy green vegetables are good sources of iron.

As you start puberty, you'll also need extra amounts of another important nutrient called zinc. Zinc and proteins work together to help you grow taller and stronger. You can get added zinc from chicken, lean meats, dairy products, and whole grains.

Don't be surprised if, these days, you're often hungry or feel wiped out when you haven't eaten. This is your body's way of telling you to give it the nutrients it depends on for proper growth. Because of all the changes your body is undergoing, it's a good idea to eat a variety of healthy foods each day. This includes plenty of fruits, vegetables, and whole grains.

 **Finding Food That's Right for You**

Interested in learning more about a diet that can help you stay healthy? The U.S. Department of Agriculture has created MyPyramid (www.mypyramid.gov) to help you figure out how to eat right and take care of your growing body. The pyramid identifies how much you should consume from six food groups: (1) Grain (2) Vegetables (3) Fruits (4) Milk (5) Meat and beans (6) Oils. Remember to keep your fat intake low because you only need a little bit to stay healthy.

MyPyramid suggests a range of servings for each major food group. The amount per day that's right for you depends on many factors, including how old you are, what you weigh, how tall you are, whether you're a boy or girl, and what your activity level is. The more active you are, the more servings you'll need. If you want more help figuring out what and how much to eat each day, talk to your doctor or school nurse.

You don't have to measure every bit of food you put in your mouth. But tracking your food intake at MyPyramid is a way to make the path to good nutrition less complicated.

## Dieting Dangers

During puberty, you may become more concerned about your weight. You're growing and changing every day, and gaining weight is a normal part of the process. One of the best things you can do for yourself is to avoid obsessing about weight and body size. It's also a good idea to avoid comparing your weight or body size to that of other people. Everybody—every *body*—is different. What's right for someone else isn't necessarily right for *you*. If you have concerns about your weight, talk to a parent and your doctor or school nurse to get more information.

Some people develop problems with eating. You may have heard or read something about eating disorders, which affect both girls and boys. There are three main types of eating disorders: *anorexia, bulimia,* and *compulsive overeating.*

A person with anorexia starves to become and stay thin and may also exercise excessively to burn off calories. Because of a distorted body image, someone with anorexia looks in the mirror and imagines fat where there isn't any. Without treatment, the person may develop severe health problems, or even die from starvation.

The main symptom of bulimia is bingeing and purging, which means eating a great deal of food, and then vomiting or taking laxatives afterward. Bulimia, like anorexia, may also involve exercising to excess. While a person with anorexia may eat very little, a person with bulimia may appear to eat normally, knowing the food will be purged. As with anorexia, severe health problems may result. People with bulimia may be at a normal weight, so it's easy to hide the condition. Since bulimia could become life-threatening, getting help is important.

Compulsive overeating, like bulimia, includes bingeing. Someone who's a compulsive overeater may eat average-sized portions in front of other people, but then binge while

> "Last year, I noticed a friend had lost a lot of weight, so I talked to her about it. She saw that I was really concerned, and she got help."
> —**Roland, 13**

alone. One result of compulsive overeating is obesity, which means being extremely overweight. During the middle school years, those who are overweight may be teased or treated as outcasts, which can lead to feelings of loneliness. Compulsive overeaters then turn to food for comfort, leading to further weight gain. Obesity is also associated with Type 2 diabetes, so that's another reason to seek help.

 ## Struggling with Weight

Not all people who struggle with their weight compulsively overeat or have other eating disorders. For many, being overweight or obese results from a combination of unhealthy food choices, oversized portions, and too little exercise. If you worry about your weight (or a parent has expressed concern), it's a good idea to talk with a health professional. This person can tell you what foods and activities are best for your health.

What all three of these disorders have in common is secrecy. Someone who has problems with food may avoid sitting in the cafeteria, disappear into the bathroom after every meal, hide food in a closet or some other place, or obsess about maintaining a certain weight for activities like wrestling, gymnastics, or ballet. If you suspect that someone you know has an eating disorder, talk to an adult you trust. If you're having problems with food, get help right away. It can feel uncomfortable to tell someone what's happening, but reaching out is the first step toward getting help and support.

**National Eating Disorders Association**
**www.nationaleatingdisorders.org**
Connect with this organization for information on eating disorders, treatment options, and support groups.

**Overeaters Anonymous**
**www.oa.org**
The website of Overeaters Anonymous is a place where people recovering from compulsive overeating can connect and support one another.

# Catch Some Zzzzzzzzz

Eating well to get all of the nutrients you need is very important. That's not all it takes to stay healthy, though. In addition to good food, your body also needs to get a lot of rest. About one-third of your life is spent sleeping—it's an essential part of life.

When you sleep, your mind and body are at rest, and this allows you to preserve the energy you'll need during the day. Most people need about eight hours of sleep each night, but during the tween and teen years, even more sleep is required. That's because during sleep your pituitary gland (located in your brain) releases large amounts of growth hormones. To grow at the highest rate possible for you, you need to get a good night's rest. You may need to take a nap after school sometimes to refresh yourself before a night of homework.

"During the school week, I have to get up at 7 a.m. I wish school would start later. Sometimes I feel like I'm drifting off in class. I do fall asleep in school once in a while, and I'm not the only one!"

**—Kevin, 13**

When you get enough sleep, you're more alert in the morning. You'll have more energy and be able to concentrate better. Experts also say that when you're sleep-deprived, you're more likely to overeat. That's one more reason to get enough rest.

# Move That Body

In addition to a healthy diet and proper sleep, physical activity is also important for staying healthy. By staying active, you help your heart, lungs, muscles, bones, and other vital body parts—even your skin and hair. Physical movement makes you think, look, and feel better, too.

Becoming fit isn't about sculpting your body into the "perfect" shape. Think of being physically active as an important part of taking good care of yourself. When you work out, focus on having fun and challenging your body.

Being fit means that:

- You can tackle the day's challenges and have plenty of energy left for play.
- Your heart, lungs, bones, and muscles are strong.
- Your body is firm and flexible.
- Your percentage of body fat is low, and your weight is within a normal range.
- You feel good about yourself and have a positive outlook on life.

If you want to be healthy and fit, and give your body the best chance to grow properly, make physical activity a regular part of your routine. Get involved in a sport (see pages 137–138 for more information) or find another type of physical activity you enjoy, such as dance, karate, biking, skateboarding, or electronic fitness games. Spend time outdoors hiking, walking your dog, or swimming. You can still enjoy television, video games, reading, the computer and other stationary activities. Just make an effort to avoid sitting for hours at a time without doing something physical.

## FAST FACT

Did you know that physical activity also increases brainpower? Studies have shown that those who are active perform better on tests. Not only that, exercise can also improve your mood. When you're active, your brain releases endorphins and other chemicals that can help you feel good.

# Keep It Clean (Your Body, That Is!)

When you reach puberty, your sweat glands also become more active. Maybe you used to be able to play basketball without breaking a sweat, but now your jump shot isn't all people are noticing. Body odor is one of the changes that may signal to you—and others—that you're going through puberty. Hormones have a lot to do with this. They affect the glands under your arms, which release some not-so-sweet-smelling chemicals when you sweat.

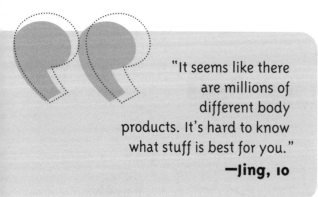

The best way to smell clean is to stay clean. Take a shower or bath every day, and wash up again after working out. Also use a deodorant or an antiperspirant. Both help mask odors, but an antiperspirant also helps to decrease the amount you sweat. Many of these products build up their effectiveness, so if you forget to put some on one day because you're late for school, you're still getting a little protection. Companies have also come up with a wide variety of body sprays, colognes, and aftershaves. If you want to use these products, get opinions from people you trust about which one might work best for you. Remember that a little goes a long way and that too much can turn people away.

As long as you're thinking about odor, consider your feet. After a few hours in sweaty sneakers, the smell of your feet might make even your closest friends keep their distance. Air out your athletic shoes after every use and sprinkle baking soda inside them to keep them fresh. Instead of wearing the same shoes to school every day, give one pair a rest and put on another pair for a day or two.

To protect your feet from a common fungus known as athlete's foot, keep them clean and dry. If you shower at school after gym, wear flip-flops or other waterproof footwear to prevent catching any fungus that's been left on the floor by someone else. Athlete's foot, which causes very itchy feet, can be treated with over-the-counter medications.

One last thing: An easy, but often forgotten, way to stay healthy and clean is by washing your hands. Get into the habit of washing up before meals, after touching dirty surfaces, and after using the bathroom. Good old soap and water help to stop the spread of germs that cause colds and serious illnesses. You might want to carry around a small container of hand sanitizer for those times when a sink and soap are not nearby.

## Stop the Invasion of the Zits

You may never have thought that much about your skin until now. Suddenly—zap!—zits are invading your face, back, and maybe even your chest. The pimples that tend to appear during puberty are the result of the oil glands in your skin increasing in both size and activity. If your skin is naturally oily, you're likely to experience more breakouts than if your skin is on the dry side. Ask your parents what their skin looked like when they were your age. Parents can pass on a tendency toward pimples or clear skin.

You can find a lot of cleansers, astringents, lotions, and medications designed to clear up pimples or acne. These products can help, and so can keeping your skin clean. Wash your face in the morning, in the evening, and after exercising. Because dirt and oil from your hair can cause pimples on your face, be sure to pull your hair back or wear a cap when you play sports. You may even want to cut your hair shorter or avoid bangs if you tend to get a lot of pimples on your forehead. Avoid picking at pimples because this will only make them worse and may infect them.

There's no absolute way to avoid a breakout, but good skincare can help lessen pimples, whiteheads, and blackheads. Some experts say that eating lots of fresh fruits and vegetables leads to clearer skin. Drinking at least six glasses of water each day can also help.

**American Academy of Dermatology**
**www.aad.org**
This site, providing information on acne and other skin conditions, can also help you find a local dermatologist.

**Skin Cancer Foundation**
**www.skincancer.org**
Visit this site for facts on skin cancer prevention and sun safety guidelines.

You may notice that on days when you're more stressed out, your skin is oilier and more prone to getting zits. You may feel better knowing that pimples don't last forever, and they're one more sign of growing up. By the end of adolescence, your skin most likely will be clearer. If you have a severe case of acne, ask about making an appointment with a dermatologist. Dermatologists specialize in skin problems and can prescribe acne medications.

Protecting your skin with sunscreen is a must when you're outdoors—even if it's cloudy. Use a product with a skin protection factor (SPF) of at least thirty. Research by the American Cancer Society has shown that to avoid sunburn, you need to reapply sunscreen frequently, particularly if you've been sweating a lot or have been swimming. If you're outdoors during the middle of the day when the sun's at its brightest, wear a hat or baseball cap to shade your face and scalp.

"This one neighbor of ours is super tan from lying out in his yard every day. My mom says she's worried he's going to get cancer."

**—Dom, 12**

Some people think that exposure to the sun helps clear up zits, plus gives light-colored skin a "healthy" tan. Unfortunately, this isn't true. When skin darkens or reddens after time in the sun, this is a sign of damage. Some people think naturally dark skin can't be harmed by the sun. Skin can freckle, darken, or burn when exposed to the sun's ultraviolet radiation (UVA and UVB rays) whether you're fair-skinned or dark, so it's best to protect yourself. Start taking good care of your skin now, and you'll thank yourself in ten, twenty, or thirty years. That's when signs of sun damage—including wrinkles, spots, or even cancer— usually show up.

## A Closing Thought...

One of the questions that middle school students often have is, "Am I normal?" Keep in mind that "normal" covers a wide range. You may be a head taller or shorter than everyone else in your class. You may have more or less body hair, zits, or muscles than your friends. You may experience wet dreams or periods long before or after others your age. You may show all the signs of puberty described in this chapter or none of them . . . yet. The bottom line is you're developing in your own way and at your own rate—and that's just the way it should be. You're a unique individual. If all of the body changes are making you wonder and ask questions, try not to worry. That's just a normal reaction to getting older!

# Like the Skin You're In

Because the middle school years include a lot of physical changes, most tweens and teens begin to think more about appearance than ever before. Feelings about looks can change from day to day, or even hour to hour. You might have doubts about how you look or even worry that appearance determines your worth as a person. But that's not true. How you look is only a small piece of who you are. You are also made up of your heart, mind, personality, thoughts, and feelings. That's not to mention all of the other unique things about you, like accomplishments, interests, experiences, talents, and dreams. If your outside package starts to seem all-important, it can help to remember all of these other great things about you. **Survival Tip #2** has many other ways to learn to like the skin you're in.

# Give Yourself a Self-Esteem Boost

Self-esteem is a measure of how you feel about yourself. If your self-esteem is strong, you can face challenges with a positive attitude and bounce back quickly after mistakes and disappointments. You believe in yourself and your ability to succeed, and that means taking positive risks and setting realistic goals. When you're proud of yourself, you feel comfortable feeling good about someone else's accomplishments, too.

On the other hand, if your self-esteem is weak, you're more likely to take negative risks and set unrealistically high or low goals. Because you don't value yourself enough, you may go along with the crowd just to fit in and feel accepted. And you may want others to fail because you think that might make you feel better about yourself. But it won't.

Having healthy self-esteem comes both from how people treat you and how you treat yourself and others. When people who matter to you show they care about you, that's a self-esteem booster. So is being treated with kindness and consideration by those you love. You can also raise your self-esteem by treating yourself and the people who are important to you with care and respect.

"I hate it when people think I'm ten years old just because I'm short."
—**Annie, 13**

"I didn't care about appearance until sixth grade, but now I spend a lot of time on how I look."
—**Manny, 14**

"I'm excited about getting braces this year. I can't wait to get rid of the big gap between my two front teeth."
—**Natasha, 12**

**Avoiding Self-Esteem Sinkers**

To keep your self-esteem healthy, you'll have to watch out for the Self-Esteem Sinkers. Don't let them pull you down!

- **Worrying about what other people think.** It takes a lot of energy to imagine what everyone's thinking of you. The real question is: What do you think of yourself?

- **Comparing yourself negatively to other people.** Remember you're unique. You can look and do things your own way.

- **Expecting to be perfect.** No one is perfect, so why try to be? You're human, which means you'll make mistakes. Learn from them, forgive yourself, and move on.

- **Playing the "I'll be happy when . . ." game.** Have you ever told yourself, "I'll be happy only if I make the team" or "I'll finally be happy when I earn an A+" or even "I can't be happy unless I get this DVD/shirt/cell phone/bike"? This is one game you can't ever win. It's a lot easier to feel happy when you appreciate what you *have* instead of worrying about what you *don't* have.

Believing in yourself can be a big challenge during the middle school years. Research shows that between the ages of ten and fourteen, many people experience *shrinking* self-esteem. This can leave tweens and teens questioning their decisions, abilities, and smarts. If this sounds like you, you might need a self-esteem boost. Here are some fun ideas to try:

**Create a list of things that make you proud.** A list like this can help remind you that you're a valuable person. Your list might include accomplishments you are proud of, unique things about you, special things you have done for others, or anything else that makes you feel good about being you. Any time you want to boost your self-esteem, read through the list or add more items to it.

**Practice visualization.** Go someplace private, close your eyes, and imagine a quality you'd like to have (or one you already have but would like to strengthen). For example, maybe you'd like to be more confident, artistic, or brave. Now imagine—or visualize—a scene in which you're showing this quality. Perhaps you'll envision yourself confidently taking a test, painting an amazing picture, or doing a trick on your skateboard. Visualization means you start with imagination and end up with a better image of yourself. You can do this any time to feel more optimistic about the future.

**Set goals.** If you want to achieve in life, start by setting goals. It's best to focus on achievements you know you can reach if you really work toward them. When you reach goals, don't forget to reward yourself and take time to recognize the progress you are making. (You can learn more about goal setting on pages 158–159.)

**Be physically active.** Activity does more than get you in shape—it also helps you feel good. Strenuous activity that gets your heart rate up releases endorphins (brain chemicals) that give you a happy, relaxed feeling. Experts say people who are active on a regular basis feel better about who they are.

**Learn to stand up for yourself.** You'll feel better about yourself if you know how to express your opinion and let your voice be heard. You don't have to allow other people to take advantage of you, tease you, or push you around. Sticking up for yourself can be a challenge, but the more you do it, the easier it gets!

**Look for inspiration.** You can find meaningful stories and quotes in books, magazines, and online. Keep reminders of these inspiring words and actions where you'll see them—like your desk, bulletin board, or mirror. You can also write about them in a journal or on your blog.

"When I'm feeling down, I go skateboarding. No matter what's bothering me, I feel a lot better after taking a ride on my board."
**—Richard, 13**

**Be Confident in Who You Are** by Annie Fox. Check out this book for graphic-novel stories and advice on feeling good about who you are.

**It's My Life!**
**www.pbskids.org/itsmylife**
This site features helpful information and advice for getting older.

# Stay Positive

Another way to feel good about who you are is to use positive thinking. Scientists have shown that thinking positive thoughts can help people feel better about themselves and be more successful in life. Unfortunately, a lot of people—including many middle school students—get in the habit of negative thinking. Maybe some of these thoughts sound familiar:

"I can't do anything right."

"What if I mess up?"

"No one likes me."

"I hate how I look."

"I'm not good enough."

Negative thinking and negative self-talk can lower your self-esteem. When your head is filled with negatives, you're less likely to take risks or achieve what you want. (Because why try anything if you've already predicted you'll fail?) Then, when you do fail, you probably tell yourself, "See, I knew I couldn't do it." This is known as a self-fulfilling prophecy.

You have the power to turn around many situations by thinking about them positively. The next time you're facing a challenge, make an effort to listen to the voice in your head. If you replace negative words with positive ones, you'll notice a difference in how you feel. And with practice, you'll get better at seeing yourself—and your life—in a brighter light. That's known as the power of positive thinking!

 **Finding Positive Thoughts**

| Situation | Instead of: | Tell yourself: |
| --- | --- | --- |
| **Before a test** | "I know I'll fail." | "I'll study hard and do my best." |
| **During class** | "If I say the wrong answer, they'll think I'm dumb." | "I'll give it my best shot. If I get the answer wrong, I'll find out why." |
| **If you make a mistake** | "I can't do anything right." | "Mistakes are a chance to learn." |
| **When you meet new people** | "They won't like me." | "We may have a lot in common." |
| **Before the school dance** | "No one will dance with me because I'm not cute enough." | "If I go with my friends, we'll have fun. Plus, I can do the asking!" |
| **When a friend or family member encourages you to try something new** | "I'm going to look bad if I can't do it right." | "It will be fun to learn a new skill." |
| **If your plans get canceled** | "Now I'll be bored the rest of the day." | "Maybe someone else can hang out." |

From now on, every time you hear that negative "inner critic" saying something that sounds like it came from your worst enemy, substitute different words. Replace negative thoughts with the kind of praise you might hear from a close friend or someone who really admires you. That's positive self-talk in action!

# Feel Good About How You Look

## FAST FACT

Staying positive can make you feel better about who you are and help you accomplish goals. But that's not all. Positive thinking has also been shown to benefit overall health, possibly even fending off the common cold! People who are optimistic are better at handling stress than those who are pessimistic (or negative).

Positive thinking can be a powerful tool to help you feel good about who you are. It can also help you feel better about how you *look*. With all the changes that go along with puberty, it's not surprising that middle school students often find it hard to feel comfortable in their own skin. Staying positive is one way to help you feel less awkward or anxious.

Still, it can be hard to feel confident about appearance. The middle school years are a time when looks can seem really important. People may talk a lot about who's cute, or cool, or well-dressed—and who's not. It might even seem like being attractive is all that really matters in life, which obviously isn't true.

"On days when my favorite clothes are in the laundry and my hair looks awful, I almost wish I could go back to bed instead of going to school."

—Steve, 11

During puberty, your image of yourself may go up and down each day. In fact, your self-image (how you see yourself) is kind of like a barometer. A barometer is an instrument that measures the pressure of the atmosphere to predict the weather. A rise in barometric pressure predicts sunny days, while a drop in pressure indicates rain. In a similar way, you might look in the mirror and like what you see one day. But suppose the very next day you get a disastrous haircut? Suddenly your image of yourself goes from sunny to cloudy.

At this point in your development, you still have more growing to do. Your face, height, weight, and almost everything else about your body will change within the next few years. You'll probably even go through what nearly everyone else in the whole world has gone through during puberty: an awkward stage. While it's normal to feel anxious about body changes you can't control, it may help to remember a few of the things that you can change. Flash the world a genuine smile, show people your kind heart, and make others laugh with your sense of humor. These are all attractive qualities that have nothing to do with appearance.

If you're feeling down about your looks, consider a few things you like about your appearance. Whatever they are, write them in a list called "My Good Points." If you can't think of anything to write, get help from a friend or someone in your family. (You may be surprised at all the positive things this person has to say!) Review your list and give yourself the credit you deserve. And instead of focusing on your so-called flaws, keep reminding yourself of your good points. With time and effort, you'll become more comfortable with your looks. And when you are, other people will feel more comfortable around you.

## Bracing for Braces

Just when you start caring a lot more about your appearance, your dentist may recommend a visit to the orthodontist. Braces aren't something to get totally stressed about. They're temporary—you won't have to wear them forever.

You may wonder if braces will hurt, whether other people will think you look weird wearing them, or if the braces will make it impossible for you to kiss anyone with confidence. Here are the facts:

- Braces hurt a little when you first get them on (and when you get them tightened).
- Your teeth may ache for a few days afterward.
- The wires take some getting used to.

Will everyone stare at your newly shiny mouth? There's no way to predict exactly how other people will react, but most likely, they'll notice the change. After a while, people will get used to seeing you in braces, and it won't be a big deal. As for kissing, that's almost always a big deal—whether you wear braces or not! (Pages 112–113 have more about kissing.)

Some people like traditional silver braces, while others prefer clear ones or colorful wires. It's up to you to choose braces that fit your style. You can even change the colors of the wires to match the season or a special holiday.

Depending on what your orthodontist recommends, you may need to wear headgear that attaches to your braces and hooks around your neck or over your head. Most likely, you can put on your headgear at night before you go to bed. Or you may need to wear small rubber bands that attach to little hooks on your braces. Usually, one rubber band connects the top wire to the bottom wire on each side of your mouth. Just be careful not to open your mouth too wide, which could cause the rubber band to break or to shoot out of your mouth.

The most important thing to know about braces is that when you have them, you have to take extra care of your teeth. Make sure you brush carefully. You may want to keep a toothbrush and toothpaste at school so you can brush after lunch. Your orthodontist may suggest a toothbrush specially designed to reach around the wires in your mouth. He or she may also tell you to stay away from sticky snacks like caramels, taffy, and licorice, which can get caught in your braces or bend the wires.

Once your braces are removed, you usually have to wear a retainer for a while. Retainers are made of plastic and sometimes combined with wire, and they're molded to the shape of your teeth. Since you probably need to remove your retainer when you eat or if you play a sport or musical instrument, make sure you don't accidentally throw it away.

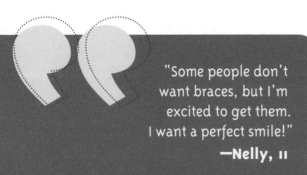

"Some people don't want braces, but I'm excited to get them. I want a perfect smile!"

**—Nelly, 11**

## Getting Glasses

You may already regularly visit an eye doctor (an ophthalmologist or an optometrist). If not, it's a good idea to start going during the middle school years. An eye doctor can help you figure out if you need to get glasses, or if you should have your current prescription adjusted. You may decide you're ready for contact lenses, and your parents and doctor can help you determine if and when these lenses are right for you. If you play sports, you may be required to wear special sports glasses or goggles for protection.

Whether you need glasses, contacts, or goggles, follow these two rules: Wear them and take care of them. Lots of people forget how important it is to put on their glasses or contacts, and keep them clean. You may sometimes think it's a pain to soak your contact lenses properly, but you need to do that regularly to prevent infection.

If you've never worn glasses before, you might be self-conscious about getting a pair. As with braces, people may notice the change and comment on it. Eventually, they'll get used to seeing you in glasses. When you go to pick out your frames, bring along a friend or two to get another opinion. It can be fun to choose glasses that express your own style!

# Develop Good Personal Habits and a Unique Style

You may notice that your hair is getting oilier, which is normal during puberty. Or that you've got a few "flakes," otherwise known as dandruff. You can use products for oily hair or a dandruff problem. You might also need to shampoo your hair more often, maybe even every day.

If you have a hairstyle that requires constant maintenance or if most of the morning is dedicated to your hair, you may want to go for a simpler style. Likewise, if you're known at school as "bedhead," you may want to put more energy into combing or brushing. (That is, unless that's your style.)

Some girls start experimenting with makeup in middle school. Using cosmetics is a personal choice, but parents usually have something to say about it. Some girls aren't allowed to use makeup until they reach a certain age. Others don't have any restrictions at all. Whether it's about makeup or a new hairstyle, think about whether changes are really right for you. You can also get opinions from family members or friends.

## A Few Words About Piercing

The middle school years are a time when you're changing quickly, and you may feel pressured to look older. Friends and other people in your class may be thinking about piercing ears, belly buttons, noses, tongues, or other body parts.

Some states have laws about how old you have to be to get your body pierced. One thing you should know is that piercing can be risky. If the procedure isn't done right, you could get an infection like hepatitis—or worse. Unskilled "piercers" could also cause nerve damage or scarring. Each type of piercing has its own dangers. Ear piercing can tear or split the earlobe. Nose studs can become buried in the skin. Tongue piercings can cause teeth fractures, swelling, bleeding, damaged cheek tissue, and lisped or slurred speech. Before you get pierced anywhere, talk to a parent about the decision. Make sure you have permission first and you understand the risks.

## What About Shaving?

Whether you're a boy or a girl, puberty is the time to make some decisions about shaving. Some boys start shaving the moment they spot a little hair on their upper lip. Other boys decide not to shave because they think they look older with a mustache, no matter how light it is.

Some girls choose to shave their underarms or legs while others prefer a natural look. Still others remove unwanted hair by waxing or using a depilatory cream with hair-removal ingredients. And some girls use a bleaching cream to lighten the hair on their upper lip or on their arms. If you want to try any of these products, be sure to read the directions carefully first. Lasers have become common for hair removal. When you're older, you might decide to give that treatment a try. Several sessions are usually needed, and it's expensive.

"I like my mustache. I think it makes me look more like a man."

**—Tran, 14**

Most people use razors to remove hair. You can choose a regular razor or an electric shaver. Following are some basic instructions for using a razor, though it's also a good idea to get help from someone who has more shaving experience than you do.

**Step #1: Choose the right razor for you.** There are a huge variety of razors to choose from. Disposables are usually plastic, and you use them a few times and then throw them away. With a cartridge razor, you keep the razor but buy new blade cartridges whenever the blade needs to be replaced. (These are better for the environment.)

What's most important is that the razor is sharp and clean. If you're out of razors or blades, don't borrow someone else's used ones—it's possible to spread skin problems or diseases.

**Step #2: Prepare your skin.** Warm water or steam from a bath or shower softens hairs, allowing them to be cut more easily. If you're not going to bathe before you shave, soak your skin with warm, soapy water.

When you're ready to shave, wet your skin with warm water and slather on some shaving cream. This shaving cream lather softens your hair and lubricates your skin, allowing the blade to glide over it smoothly.

This is a key step for a good shave. If you skip over the prep work, you might look and feel like you shaved with a cheese grater!

**Step #3: Use the proper technique.** Use a light, slow stroke while moving the razor along the surface of your skin. Keep your razor clean as you're using it—rinse it often in warm water to remove clumps of hair or shaving cream.

**Step #4: Clean up afterward.** After you've finished shaving, rinse the area with cool water and pat it dry. If you want to use some kind of lotion afterward, avoid alcohol-based products, which can sting or irritate freshly shaven skin. If you're going to use your blade again, rinse it thoroughly and shake off any excess water.

Small cuts are bound to happen the first couple of times you shave. If you're bleeding, you can apply a styptic pencil. These white, chalky "pencils" are sort of old-fashioned and they sting when you apply them, but they work. Or you can use a tried-and-true remedy: tear a tiny piece of tissue paper and stick it on the cut. After a few minutes, moisten the paper and gently peel it off. Don't forget, or you'll end up leaving the house with little pieces of tissue sticking to your skin.

## Clothing Matters

Fashions come and go. What's in one day is often out the next. You probably have your own sense of style. Maybe you often try to match your clothing to that of your friends or the people you see on TV. Wanting to look cool is okay, but becoming obsessed with getting a certain jacket or pair of jeans isn't a good idea. This is especially true when clothes are expensive and might be beyond the budget of your family. The good news is there are plenty of ways to find a look that's right for you without spending a fortune.

- Wear layers (a T-shirt over another shirt, for example), and try different combinations to give your wardrobe more variety.
- Visit a thrift store or consignment shop for good deals on used clothing.
- Raid a family member's closet (with permission) to find something different to wear.
- Accessorize: ties, scarves, buttons, belts, hats, socks, pins, and other accessories are an inexpensive way to make a fashion statement.
- Hold a clothing swap party (with parent permission) for a group of friends. Set ground rules, such as taking the same number of items you brought and only bringing clothing in good condition.

**Get the Scoop on Celebrities**

You probably look up to actors, models, musicians, and sports stars—many people do. But the admiration may turn into something more. You might feel like you have to look like a celebrity to look good. Here's the truth behind all the glamour:

- **Celebrities** have "tricks" for making themselves more attractive, such as using fashion consultants, makeup artists, hairstylists, and plastic surgeons. In addition, many celebrities diet or exercise way too much in pursuit of thinner bodies.

- **Television actors** and **models** rely on professionally applied makeup, special lighting, and flattering camera angles. If you saw these people in person, the makeup on their faces would look strange.

- **Magazine models** have their photos touched up and improved by computer technology. Computers can subtract pounds and completely change the look of people's hair, eyes, and skin.

- **Professional athletes** spend tremendous amounts of time building their bodies with the help of trainers, team doctors, and other professionals who monitor the athletes' weight, health, and fitness level.

Another way to help keep a full wardrobe is to care for what you wear. Your clothes may see a lot of wear and tear, which is why it can help to learn to make some simple repairs. Ask an adult at home to teach you how to sew on a button or fix a split seam. You can also find out how to use the washer, the dryer, and an iron if you don't know how already. Then simply follow the laundering and ironing instructions on the clothing labels. Taking care of your own laundry not only gives your parents a break but also guarantees your clothes will be clean and ready to wear when you need them.

Some tweens and teens put a lot of energy into their looks, spending extra money on clothes, shoes, jewelry, and other accessories. It can be fun to try out different styles and fashions. But sometimes you might feel pressured to look like an adult. You might also feel pressure to wear certain brands of clothing—to avoid being labeled or teased. Lots of girls and guys are brand-conscious and feel anxious about owning the right clothes and shoes.

It's easy to get caught up in comparing your own clothes, shoes, watch, haircut, and cell phone to everyone else's. But all of this is only as big of a deal as you make it. Stuff is just stuff. Having more or less of it doesn't make you more or less of a person.

Many people out there want you to be preoccupied with material items. Marketers, ad writers, product developers, magazine editors, and owners of popular clothing stores want to sell you things: clothes, shoes, hair products, body sprays. Basically, they're trying to sell you an image.

Teen magazines are filled with fashion advice, beauty tips, and articles on how and how not to dress. These magazines also contain tons of clothing advertisements, all of which are sending you some very strong messages about how to look. Even if you don't read these magazines, you're probably seeing lots of appearance-related ads on TV or online—maybe hundreds of ads every day! These ads come through all forms of media: newspapers, television, websites, billboards, DVDs, video games, magazines, and movies.

Just for fun, try the following activity with a friend. Ask the adults at home if you can see old yearbooks from their high school days. You may be surprised by who was considered attractive. You can also go to your local library and look at old issues of fashion and beauty magazines. Take a look at the clothes, hairstyles, shoes, and fashion advice. Seeing these outdated images can reveal that styles really are here today and gone tomorrow. In the future, anyone glancing at pictures of what's considered cool today will probably wonder why everyone had such bizarre taste!

## A Closing Thought . . .

If you've ever expressed doubts about your appearance, maybe your parents or other adults in your life responded with, "Looks don't matter that much." And if looks don't really matter, you might have wondered why so many adults seem preoccupied with their appearance. To confuse matters, people on TV and in movies and magazines receive extensive makeovers to make themselves more attractive. The message you're receiving from them is, "Looks do matter."

So, what are you supposed to believe? The answer: believe in yourself.

Sure, looks matter somewhat—otherwise why would people bother to wash, shave, fix their hair, put on attractive clothes, or do anything to improve their appearance? Taking good care of your body, skin, hair, and teeth are all positive steps toward looking and feeling your best. But another important step is staying positive about who you are.

# Understand Your Feelings

Stormy. Changing. Extreme. These words may describe weather, but they can also apply to moods. Mood swings are common during the middle school years. People often blame hormones for the emotional ups and downs of adolescence. Hormones play a part in how you feel, but research shows they're not the only cause of mood swings. Added responsibilities at home and at school can contribute, as can troubles with friends or fitting into the social scene. You probably expect more from yourself, too. All of these pressures can be tough to handle and make you feel frustrated. Sometimes strong emotions might surprise or even frighten you. **Survival Tip #3** is all about how you can understand moods and deal with feelings in helpful ways.

# What Are You Feeling?

How you feel has a lot to do with what is happening around you. It's natural to feel upset when something bad happens or nervous when there's a new challenge around the corner. Just imagine yourself in these situations and think about how you might feel.

- The referee makes a bad call against you, and you foul out of the game.

- Your teacher says, "I'm going to have to call your parents if you continue to do poorly on your tests."

- You hear your dad tell your sister how proud he is of her grades.

- Your mom says you have to go to bed right now, but your favorite TV show won't be over for another twenty minutes.

- You're changing for gym with your classmates in the locker room.

- The recital is about to begin. Your entire family and all of your friends are in the audience waiting to watch you.

"I have a learning disability, and it gets frustrating when I'm trying hard and my parents don't seem to believe me."
—**Josh, 11**

"Sometimes, when my teacher calls on me in class, I get really nervous and forget everything."
—**Kyra, 13**

"I keep my feelings inside. My friends and I don't talk about feelings. We just don't."
—**Devin, 12**

"I like playing basketball on a travel team, but it can also be very stressful. My coaches and teammates expect me to score a lot of points every game."
—**Alicia, 14**

Maybe these don't apply to you, but other situations leave you feeling upset or excited. One way to help you understand your feelings and your moods is to write about them. You might write in a journal or work on the computer. Start by writing the date, what you're feeling, and why you think you feel this way. You might also write about things you can do to feel better when you're down.

You may already keep a journal so that writing about feelings comes naturally. Or it might feel weird to write about your feelings, especially if you're worried that someone might read what you wrote. You don't have to show your words to anyone unless you want to. Keep your journal in a place that only *you* know about, like in the back of your closet or even in a trunk or safe that has a lock on it. If you write on the computer, create password-protected files or store them on a memory stick and keep it in a private place. This way, you won't have to worry about anyone sneaking a peek.

If you're not the writing type, another good way to deal with your feelings is by talking about them. You might have a conversation with a friend or someone else you're close to. Sometimes, it's best to go to an adult, especially if you're feeling really confused, hurt, or alone. You can talk with a parent, teacher, counselor, coach, school nurse, or youth group leader—someone you trust who will listen to you and give you solid support and good advice.

**Get the Conversation Going**

Below are some ways you can start important, but difficult, conversations:

- "This is hard for me to talk about but . . ."
- "I need to talk about some things I'm feeling right now."
- "I'm feeling uncomfortable about sharing this . . ."
- "Sometimes I feel so (angry, sad, upset, worried) that I don't know what to do. Can you give me some advice?"
- "Is this a good time for us to talk about something important?"
- "I need to share something that's bothering me."

You can adapt conversation openers to suit your own personal style. The important thing is to start that conversation. It may seem difficult to talk about your feelings, but most likely, the adult you've chosen to open up to will try to make it easier for you. You picked that person because you trust her or him. Once you've started to talk, the hardest part of the conversation will be behind you.

*Getting to Know the Real You: 50 Fun Quizzes Just for Girls* by Harriet S. Mosatche and Elizabeth K. Lawner. Filled with fun quizzes, this book offers tips on self-esteem, stress, and other important topics.

*The Teenage Guy's Survival Guide: The Real Deal on Girls, Growing Up, and Other Guy Stuff* by Jeremy Daldry. This honest, entertaining book about getting older is written by a guy who's been there.

# How Embarrassing!

Everyone feels embarrassed from time to time. No matter how hard someone tries to be smooth and sophisticated, it's impossible to avoid slipping up now and then. For example, it's embarrassing to find out you've been talking to someone you have a crush on with a piece of bright green lettuce stuck to your front tooth! Or to realize, in the middle of telling a joke about your science teacher, that she's *standing right behind you.* One of the best ways to survive an embarrassing moment is to say, "Whoa, am I embarrassed!" and laugh about it. This often works better than pretending nothing happened or trying to hide what you're feeling. Laughing at mistakes can help them seem smaller.

Tweens, teens, parents, teachers—*everyone* makes mistakes and has embarrassing moments. Even celebrities, presidents, and Olympic-winning athletes. It's not the end of the world, even though it may seem like that at the time.

Think about how you usually react when someone else has an embarrassing moment. Do you double over with laughter? Do you tease the person about it? When you see someone else make a mistake, do what you can to smooth it over. That's what you'd want somebody else to do for you.

> "At a music festival, one of my friends poured water on my pants. Then when we stood up, he yelled 'Mike, that's what a Porta Potty is for!' At least fifty people turned around to look at me!"
>
> **—Mike, 13**

> "I had just started practicing some hip-hop jazz moves when I caught a glimpse of my brother's friend who had just come into the house looking for him. To make matters worse, all I was wearing was a swimsuit!"
>
> **—Ali, 12**

# Coping with Stress

*Beep! Beep! Beep!* The alarm clock startles you awake. You can't find your favorite shirt, your brother gets to the bathroom first and locks the door (and he's not going to rush for you), your father's scrambling because he's late for work, and your little sister spills milk all over your English assignment. It's not even eight in the morning, and already you're feeling completely stressed out. Sound familiar?

Many middle schoolers feel anxious about body changes, friendships, grades, tests, and family situations. It can be interesting to ask friends and family members what causes them to feel stressed. You might find that you worry about many of the same things. Maybe some of the answers you hear will also surprise you. Either way, it can be reassuring to know you're not the only one who feels anxious about some things.

Stress causes natural physical reactions in your body. While not every person has the exact same reactions, the following ones are common:

- Digestion slows so the blood can flow where it's most needed. Your mouth may get dry, or you might get a stomachache.
- More blood goes to your brain. Your face may flush or you may get a pressure headache.
- You get butterflies in your stomach because your body is producing chemicals like adrenaline, which boost your energy.
- Your heart beats harder and faster to bring oxygen-rich blood to your body.
- The blood rushes to your large muscles, decreasing the blood flow in your hands and feet. This makes them feel cooler or cold.
- You get sweaty all over, and your hands may get clammy.

Experts say parents can pass on a tendency to react in an anxious or calm way. Although your genes play a role in your anxiety level, so do other factors. Over the years, you've probably learned to deal with stressful events in certain ways. Maybe you've watched how your mom, dad, or other adults handle stress, and you've learned from them. Or maybe very early on in life you developed your own methods for coping.

> "I get stressed about tests. No matter how much I study, my brain seems to freeze when a test starts."
> **—Jenna, 12**

It's normal to have some stress in your life—everyone does. And in some ways stress can be good for you. Think about what it would be like if your school assignments could be turned in on any old date. Or if during athletic events, all the players took as much time as they wanted and never pushed themselves to do their best. What would life be like if no one ever had to set goals, study, take tests, speak before an audience, or perform in any way? Pretty dull, don't you think? Without the extra energy good stress produces, people wouldn't have as much motivation to try new things.

Even positive events—like birthdays, vacations, special holidays—can cause stress. But again, this kind of stress can feel pretty good, like an adrenaline rush, adding excitement to your life.

But some stress is definitely negative. For example, what if you're dealing with a bully, a divorce in the family, a fight with a friend, poor grades, or some other difficulty? These kinds of challenges are tough to handle and can be a huge source of stress. Sometimes you may feel ready to explode. Here are some healthy ways to help you feel better:

**Stay physically active.** Whether you're playing a competitive game of ping pong or kayaking around a lake, physical activity is a good way to relax when you're feeling stressed. Regular exercise also has been shown to improve mood.

**Eat right.** Eating healthy foods is an important way to lower your stress level. Try also to avoid caffeine. This chemical gives you an energy boost that can increase your stress level and then make you feel tired. Coffee, tea, soda, and chocolate usually contain caffeine.

## FAST FACT

Experiencing stress over a long period of time may negatively affect the immune system. With so much energy devoted to the stress response, the body loses some of its ability to fight off infection and disease.

**Get enough sleep.** Studies show that sleep deprivation can make it more difficult to handle life's stresses. Try going to bed earlier to help keep stress levels low.

**Laugh it up.** Research shows that laughter helps people feel happier. Lessen your stress by viewing funny videos online, reading humor books, or watching film comedies.

**Have some fun.** Doing something fun can take your mind off your stress. What do you like to do? Who do you enjoy spending time with? Find these people and soak up their positive energy.

**Use your problem-solving skills.** Using your energy to worry about a problem can cause more stress. Instead of feeling helpless, figure out the steps you need to take to work things out. Check out pages 89–91 for conflict-resolution tips, and pages 143–145 for help in making decisions.

**Do a relaxation exercise.** This kind of exercise involves breathing deeply and imagining a peaceful scene. Try the one on page 54. Or you can design a different one that's right for you.

**Boys Town National Hotline**
**1-800-448-3000**
This 24/7 hotline connects you with a professional counselor who will listen and provide advice on stress and other topics.

**TeenGrowth**
**www.teengrowth.com**
Check out this website for information on many health topics and advice for dealing with stress that can come with adolescence.

# TIPS  When to Get Help

How do you usually deal with stress? Maybe you listen to music, play with a pet, take a warm bath, or watch funny videos online. These are positive ways to cope. On the other hand, maybe you try to deal with stress in some not-so-positive ways. When you're anxious, do you do too much of the following things?

- eat
- sleep
- skip meals
- watch TV
- play video or computer games
- browse the Internet
- stay in your room alone
- put off things you need to do, like homework or chores

If stress is causing you to spend a lot of time by yourself or withdraw from people and activities you used to care about, it's important to talk to an adult right away. You can get this person's help finding positive ways to deal with challenges in your life. You might start by using some of the suggestions in this section.

 **Relaxation Exercise**

When you don't have much time, try using your imagination to relax. Close your eyes and imagine a scene that's peaceful and quiet—like a sunny beach or another place you find calming. Keep your eyes closed as you allow yourself to feel more relaxed.

When you have a bit more time, go through the following steps, beginning at your toes and slowly working your way up your body. If you can get someone to read the instructions to you, the exercise can be even more relaxing.

1. Tense your toes and hold for a count of five. Breathe in deeply and, as you exhale, feel your toes relaxing.

2. Keep breathing while you tense your calf muscles. Hold for a count of five. Let go of the tension in those muscles.

3. Tense both legs, including your thighs. Keep the tension for a count of five, and then release it.

4. Squeeze your buttocks and stomach muscles. Hold the tension for a count of five. Then slowly relax those muscles.

5. Next, breathe in as you tighten your fingers. Keep the tension in your fingers as you count to five. Relax your hands as you exhale.

6. Move on to your arms. Feel both arms tightening up. Count to five and release all the tension.

7. Tense your chest while you squeeze your shoulder blades together. Keep the tension for a count of five, and then relax as you exhale.

8. Move now to your jaw and cheek muscles, again tensing for five seconds and then releasing the tension.

9. Focus on your eyes and forehead, squeezing tightly for five seconds. Then feel the tension leave your face.

10. Finally, inhale deeply and, as you exhale, imagine any remaining tension leaving your body. How do you feel?

# Facing Your Fears

At this point in your life, you are probably dealing with challenges that might make you feel uncertain. These are some very common day-to-day fears:

**Speaking in public.** A lot of students feel really nervous when they have to speak in class, even if they know the correct answer. And giving an oral report can be absolute torture for some. Public speaking is also one of the most common fears among adults.

**Being different.** Maybe you worry you won't fit in with other people. Or you might be afraid of doing or saying something that people—particularly the "cool" crowd—will make fun of.

**Having something terrible happen.** Maybe you fear losing someone you care about, getting into an accident, or becoming sick. Or maybe you're afraid of death. Many adults are fearful about these things, too.

**Not doing well in school.** Many students worry a lot about tests, homework, projects, and grades. Some live in constant fear of not doing well in school. This fear may particularly affect students who feel the need to be perfect or who have learning difficulties.

**Having your friends turn against you.** Do you ever worry your friends will suddenly stop liking you? That they'll find a "better" friend to hang out with? Because friendships are so important during the middle school years, this kind of fear is common. (Your friends are probably feeling the very same way!)

**Not being liked by your teacher.** At the beginning of the school year, some students are afraid their teachers won't like them. Some students who feel this way might be worried about succeeding in school. Others may have had problems with teachers in the past, and they could be concerned they'll have more issues in the new school year.

**Being embarrassed by your family.** This is a prime age for being embarrassed by your family—especially parents. Parents may mean well but say or do things that make you cringe (like reminding you to brush your teeth when your friends are over or giving you a hug and kiss in front of everyone at school).

**Trying new things.** Have you ever been afraid to try something because you were worried you wouldn't be able to do it well? Maybe you felt uncertain about joining a sports team or trying out for the school play. Many tween and teens feel this way about new experiences. Unfortunately, these fears prevent some people from *ever* challenging themselves. But how will they know how good they are at something without trying it?

# 4 Steps to Face Your Fears

Having fears is a part of life, but that doesn't mean you have to let them stop you. Here are four steps you can use to face your fears:

1. **Look at the feelings behind the fear.** Suppose you're afraid your best friend will stop spending time with you to get in with the "popular" group. Ask yourself: What is my fear based on? What else am I feeling? Are you worried you and your friend don't really share the same interests anymore? Do you feel you're not as cool or as much fun as other people? Do you think your friend is changing in ways you're not? Chances are, you're feeling more than fear.

2. **Ask yourself if the fear is realistic.** In other words, is it likely to happen or not? Using the example above, think about whether it's realistic that your friend might desert you. Has your friend done anything like that in the past? Is your friend ignoring you or showing any other signs of abandoning you? If not, the fear probably isn't realistic.

3. **Talk to an adult you trust.** If you keep your fears locked inside, they may start to seem much bigger than they really are. An adult might be able to help you figure out what your fear is based on and whether it's realistic or not.

4. **Face it!** Once you've identified your fear and you understand it a little better, you can face it head on. Start by making a step-by-step plan of action. You can track your progress using a chart similar to the following one. Decide what small step you can take first, and then figure out the next bigger step to follow. Determine what further steps to take from there.

"I want to try out for the school musical, but I'm afraid. What if my voice sounds bad at tryouts?"

**—Trent, 11**

## Taking Small Steps

Making an action plan can help you face fears by taking small steps. Here's an example of how:

**My fear:** I'm afraid to do the big class presentation that's required next month.

**What it's based on:** If I look and act nervous, everyone will know I am. I want to be accepted. I want people to think I'm more confident than I really am.

|  | Action | When | How I Felt |
|---|---|---|---|
| **Step 1** | Raise my hand during class and ask questions. | Tuesday in social studies class. Thursday during science. | Relieved I did it. |
| **Step 2** | Start practicing my report out loud at home. | Three times this week. | A little more confident each time. |
| **Step 3** | Rehearse part of my report in front of my family. | Saturday evening after dinner. | Excited—they said it was good! |

Tackling fears isn't always easy, so you may have to be patient with yourself. For example, you might have to do the steps more than one time before your fear lessens. Ask friends, family members, or trusted adults for help in designing a plan and supporting you as you carry it out.

# Dealing with Anger

Some people scream and yell when they're angry, while others get very quiet. And still others show their anger in hidden ways. They may spread rumors about the person they're mad at or plot revenge. Whether it comes on suddenly or slowly builds inside you, anger can make you feel out of control.

Getting mad once in a while is okay; anger is part of being human. Shouting at people doesn't work, though, and neither does acting out in violence. Giving someone the silent treatment is not very effective either. Here are some tips for resolving anger in healthy ways:

**Do something physical.** Anger produces a lot of extra energy in your body. It makes you feel like you want to yell or even use your fists. If you're so mad you can barely think straight, run around outside, play an electronic fitness game, practice karate kicks, go skateboarding, or turn up the volume and dance like crazy in your room.

**Take a moment to calm down.** It might not always be possible to do something physical, especially if you're in class or in the car. What can you do then? Calm down by closing your eyes and taking a long, slow, deep breath through your nose, slowly counting to five. Then breathe out through your nose, slowly counting backwards from five. Repeat this a few times until you feel more peaceful.

**Tell yourself not to let anger get the best of you.** Sometimes people don't even know they've done something to anger you. For example, maybe someone accidentally bumps you while you're carrying your lunch tray, causing your drink to spill. Is that going to ruin your day? You can choose to put your anger behind you and move on. Get your mind off your anger by thinking about something positive.

**Express your anger.** Like other feelings, anger needs to be expressed. You can write about your emotions or talk to a friend.

**Tell the person you're angry with how you feel.** You may feel uncomfortable telling someone you're angry, but it's worth it. Or you may feel that it's easier to ignore the issue or stop speaking to the person, but do you know what happens if you do? The anger stays with you, even if it's buried deep inside.

**Do something fun.** Replaying a situation that made you angry won't help you feel better. But doing something you enjoy will. Whether it's playing a computer game or reading a graphic novel, think of something that will take your body and mind to another place.

**CHECK IT OUT**

*Hot Stones and Funny Bones: Teens Helping Teens Cope with Stress and Anger* by Brian Seaward and Linda Bartlett. Featuring insight from teens around the country, this book highlights positive ways to deal with anger, frustration, and stress.

**TeensHealth**
**www.teenshealth.org**
Visit this site for general information on health as well as good advice for handling sadness, anxiety, and other strong feelings.

# Sadness and Grief

When you're sad, you might feel like your heart is broken or empty, or you just can't cope with what's going on. Unfortunately, sad things happen in life, and everyone experiences hurt and disappointment. Events like divorce, moving, a family illness, or changing schools can all cause sadness. So can losing a pet you love.

Sadness, like other emotions, eventually passes. But knowing this may not be a comfort when you're sad. One way to release sadness is through tears. Crying is your body's way of letting out painful feelings.

When you were younger, you cried often to express your feelings and needs. Now that you're older, you're probably more self-conscious about letting people see your tears. If you're a boy, you may have gotten the message "Boys don't cry." And whether you're a boy or girl, you may think crying isn't mature. Actually, crying is a healthy way to let out your feelings. You may cry if you feel sad or angry, or even if you're watching a sentimental movie. No one is ever too grown up to shed some tears.

You can handle sadness in many other ways as well. Talk to someone who can give you support—a friend, parent, teacher, or school counselor. Express your feelings in your journal, too, or through music, art, or poetry. Get outdoors to exercise and breathe some fresh air. Sometimes what you need most is a hug or a shoulder to cry on—don't be afraid to reach out to someone you love.

One of the saddest times of all is when somebody you feel close to dies—perhaps a grandparent or another family member, a friend or a friend's parent, a classmate or teacher at school, or a beloved pet. At first, you may not even believe something so terrible has happened because the pain of the loss is almost unbearable. Or you may be so upset that your emotions shut down. Everybody grieves differently. The important thing is to talk to someone about what you're going through.

Many people have their first experience with death during the middle school years, be it the loss of a pet or a person they love. The result is a tangle of emotions—sadness, grief, confusion, guilt, anger, and even fear. If you've lost a loved one or someone else who was important to you, it's normal to start questioning why life is so unfair or why people have to die. You may have lots of questions that are too big to answer on your own. Find out how you can talk with a religious advisor, a counselor, or someone else who's trained to help people deal with their sadness. You don't have to go through the pain of loss alone.

Sometimes people experience a sadness that doesn't seem to be related to a specific event. If you're unhappy and the feeling hangs on for a long time, you might be depressed. Tweens and teens can get depression, just like adults. Some signs of depression may include:

- feeling helpless or hopeless
- having trouble sleeping or feeling tired all the time
- a sadness that goes on and on
- feeling very angry with yourself or others
- being excessively anxious

If this sounds like what you're going through, get help right away. Talk to a trusted adult or call one of the hotline numbers listed below or on page 52.

*Healing Your Grieving Heart for Teens: 100 Practical Ideas* by Alan Wolfelt.
Pick up this book to find activities that can be helpful in making it through difficult times.

**Hopeline**
**1-800-784-2433**
This crisis hotline is for people who are depressed or suicidal. If you or someone you know needs help, call anytime of day or night to be connected with a crisis center.

# Helping Friends with Their Feelings

Your friends are going through many of the same physical and emotional changes you are. And, at times, your friends may feel confused, sad, or stressed. What can you do to help? If your friends ask for advice, you can offer ideas that worked for you. Otherwise, just listen and let them know you care.

If the situation seems serious, suggest they talk to an adult to get some help. You can also give your friends hotline numbers or the names of organizations that deal with the kinds of problems your friends are facing.

If a friend tells you something secret or private, what should you do? It depends on the situation. Friends need to be able to trust each other. That's just a basic rule of friendship. So if a friend tells you a secret, it's a good idea to keep it to yourself. Otherwise, you could lose your friend's trust—or even the friendship.

However, if a friend tells you something private but is in danger (for example, he or she is being abused, has an eating disorder, is suicidal, or is depressed), get help from an adult right away. These are the kinds of problems that are too serious to handle alone—no matter how smart you are or how much you care. Getting adult help for a friend who needs it is *not* a break in trust! It's the best thing you can do for both of you.

## A Closing Thought . . .

At this time in your life, you no longer think of yourself as a child. You're more mature and better able to handle your problems on your own. You probably want other people to see you as grown up and capable of taking care of yourself. As a result, you might sometimes be tempted to hide your emotions or pretend you're feeling fine when you're not. But the truth is that talking honestly about how you feel is a sign of maturity. It shows those around you that you are getting better at dealing with feelings and taking care of yourself.

# Connect with Your Family

In middle school, family relationships are changing. Parents* might like music, movies, or activities that seem weird or boring to you. Maybe they do embarrassing things, like hug or kiss you in front of your friends. It might seem like *parents* are suddenly different, but more likely what's changing is how you relate to each other and get along. Although you still need your parents, you're more independent now. As you pull away, they might try to pull you closer or have a hard time letting go. Sometimes your relationship with them might feel like a tug-of-war. You may be pulling at different ends of a rope, but there's still a connection between you. That's what **Survival Tip #4** is all about: staying connected!

*When you see the word *parents,* you can think of the adults who are responsible for you, whether that is one or two parents, another adult relative, a stepfamily, a foster family, or other people.

# Keeping Open the Lines of Communication

Communication with parents often becomes more difficult during the middle school years. That's because you've entered a new stage of development. You now have more opinions and ideas, and different needs. You probably want to be part of adult conversations and family decisions. You're older and you'd like your voice to be heard.

Adolescence is the time when you begin to establish your own interests, and your likes and dislikes. That's part of figuring out who you are (your identity). You may also be discovering ways you're different from your parents. Some conflict with your family is bound to happen as you work on your own identity.

Although you love your parents, you may now have doubts about their rules and how they run things at home. Having occasional disagreements is normal. But in some families, arguments happen often and ordinary conversations can turn into battles. Family members may say

"My mom is so busy it's hard to have good conversations with her."
—**LeShawn, 11**

"My two younger siblings are both greedy for attention, and I get left out."
—**Rissa, 14**

"Even when I do my best to speak politely, my stepdad says I'm acting out or being difficult. He gets mad at me instead of listening to what I have to say."
—**Alex, 13**

"My dad doesn't seem to ever listen; he always seems kind of preoccupied. And my brother always wants the attention all on him. I feel like no one notices me!"
—**Julie, 12**

hurtful words or have trouble talking. Communication problems make it hard to get along.

To make matters more difficult, you're at an age when you may not be comfortable showing affection for parents. They may see this as a sign that you don't care about them or need them as much as you once did. (Even if you don't really feel that way.)

## 7 Ways to Get Along with Family Members

Even though disagreements are a normal part of family life, communicating honestly and openly can be helpful in resolving conflicts. Here are some tips to try:

**Use I-messages.** These are statements that rely on the word *I* to communicate. For example, "I feel angry when I get yelled at" or "I feel that you sometimes treat me like a child, and I want to show you how responsible I can be." Instead of placing blame on the other person, I-messages focus on feelings and help defuse tense situations.

**Speak in a calm voice.** Talking calmly and politely shows respect for your family and gives you a better chance of being heard. If you scream, your parents will probably react to your tone of voice rather than to what you're saying. Showing respect can help you get respect.

**Say what you mean in a direct way.** Gather up your courage, and then make your point or ask your question. If you're worried about hurting someone's feelings or not getting the answer you want, remember that I-messages are a helpful way to communicate. Try again, using I to start off each sentence.

"Sometimes my dad says I have a bad attitude—even when I'm not doing anything wrong."
**—Marceline, 12**

**Be aware of what others feel.** Everyone has a point of view, so let each person have a say. Suppose your parents make a rule about not letting you hang out with your friends on school nights. Consider your parents' point of view.

Maybe they think you won't get your homework done if you're spending too much time with friends. Show them that you understand this, and they'll be more likely to listen to your side of the story.

**Be open to a little give and take.** One way to solve a problem is by compromising—each person gives a little to get a little. Using the previous example, what could you do to compromise? Suppose you make sure your homework is done before you go out with your friends, and you agree to be home before 8 p.m.? That may be a solution everyone can agree on.

**Pay attention to body language.** Body language is a way of communicating without words. Suppose you yell at your dad, and he asks for an apology. You say you're sorry, but cross your arms and roll your eyes. What your dad "hears" is, "I'm not a bit sorry!" Be aware of your facial expressions, your gestures, and your posture. Also, try to make eye contact to show you're paying attention.

**Work on listening.** During a disagreement or conversation, people sometimes tune each other out. Or they focus on what they're going to say next. Learning to listen takes practice and patience. But other people feel they're being treated with respect when they know you're really listening—and that makes them more likely to listen to you.

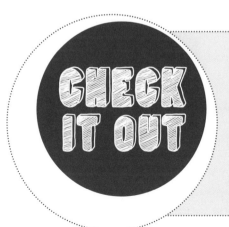

**It's My Life—Family**
**www.pbskids.org/itsmylife/family**
Visit this website for helpful advice on getting along with siblings and adults at home.

*What's Up with My Family?* by Annie Fox. This book features graphic-novel stories about being part of a family and real-life advice that can help make life at home better.

# Hot Button Issues at Home

No matter how hard family members try to get along and communicate in positive ways, some conflicts are bound to come up at home. This is especially true when it comes to hot button issues—topics that middle school students and parents often disagree about. These can include:

- homework
- chores
- television watching
- rules about curfew and bedtime
- allowance
- clothing, makeup, and other "looks stuff"
- choice of friends
- messy rooms
- privacy
- time online and texting

Family hot buttons are part of the tug-of-war between you and your parents. You want to be treated as a grown-up; they want you to act more grown-up. So, in a way, you have the same goal in mind. Hot button issues are conflicts over what being grown-up really means. You want more *freedom*. Adults at home want you to be more *responsible*.

## Rules, Rules, and More Rules

Because you're not yet an adult, your parents still have control over many parts of your life. At the same time, you're growing up, and you're better able to make decisions now. You're old enough to choose what activities to pursue, what to wear, who you spend time with, what you do on weekends, and more. But your parents still want to have their say. And they may say a lot about your choices of clothing, friends, and activities. That's because, more than anything, they want what's best for you.

But sometimes it might seem like parents are being over-protective. Just when you want more freedom to explore the world and discover your place in it, they seem to be holding you back. The best way to get more freedom? Be responsible! If you'd like to be able to do more—stay up later, go places with friends, spend some of your money on whatever you want—then you need to prove to your family that you can handle your freedom.

> "Being the youngest is a pain. My older brothers get to do whatever they want, but my mom says I have to be home by eight every night—even on weekends."
> —Jakob, 12

Suppose your parents drop you off at the mall to spend time with your friends. They're trusting you to be responsible. What happens if, a few hours later, your parents return to pick you up and you're nowhere to be found? Or what if you decide to go to a friend's house after school, and you forget to call home first? If you break their trust, your parents might believe you can't handle freedom or responsibility. The result? They may limit you even more. But if you're on time or you remember to call, your parents will know you can handle your greater freedom and probably will reward you with more.

## Chores at Home

Chores can be another major source of disagreement at home. It's not news that few people actually *enjoy* doing chores around the house. But if you think about it, most people also have a problem with eating at a sticky table covered in old pancake syrup or living without clean laundry. Who, for example, enjoys spending half an hour looking for a favorite T-shirt, only to find it's still in the laundry?

While chores may not be fun or glamorous, they definitely do help things go better at home. And they don't have to be too difficult if everyone pitches in. Think about the chores at your home and whether they are distributed fairly among family members. You can do this by creating a Chore Chart. First, list each chore that needs to be done each day or week. Next, create columns where you can write in who does each task, how much time it takes, and how difficult or unpleasant it is to do. (You might create a rating system where emptying the dishwasher is a "1" and cleaning a toilet is a "5.")

When you've finished the chart, add up all the hours each person spends on household tasks. Who does the most? Who does the least? Which family members are responsible for most of the difficult work? Is there a way to help lighten their loads? If you're already doing too much, are there helpful changes you can discuss with parents?

## Screen Time

Another common source of conflicts at home is the amount of time tweens and teens spend watching television, using a computer, playing video games, texting, or connecting with friends on social networking sites. Many people underestimate their screen time. You might start out playing a video game or browsing the Internet and before you know it, an hour has gone by. Or you might turn on the television to watch one show but not turn off the TV until after you've also watched three or four more. You used to send just a few texts a day—now you're going back and forth so many times with friends, you've lost count.

One interesting activity to try is tracking your screen time for a week. Keep track of the number of hours you spend watching TV, playing video games, and searching the Internet. Don't forget to include the time you spend connecting by phone with texts and updating social media. Before you begin, make a prediction and then see how close you get to your guess. If adults at home think you spend too much time in front of screens, you might also get them involved. Use what you learn about your media habits to start a conversation with them about how much is too much.

## FAST FACT

Many experts believe that spending too much time browsing the Internet and playing video games can have real-life consequences. People who focus most of their attention on virtual environments become isolated from others. Limited physical activity can also contribute to poor health and obesity.

## TIPS  Free Time . . . Unplugged

If you find that your screen time takes up more hours than you'd like, think about what else you could have been doing with your time. Here are some sample ideas:

- reading a book, magazine, or newspaper
- starting a new hobby or practicing a sport
- writing in a journal or creating art

Come up with other ideas to add to this list. Some of them might involve family activities, such as hiking, going on a picnic, cooking together, or just talking.

# Privacy

Privacy is a major issue during the middle school years. At this stage of your life, you need your own space. That's part of the struggle for independence. Parents and siblings may not realize that having time alone is important to you. They might forget to knock on the door before entering the room. Maybe they also look through or borrow your things without asking. It can feel like a really big deal if someone invades your privacy, especially when it comes to someone reading a private journal, emails, or text messages.

Talk to family members about making a privacy contract. You can create an agreement yourself or ask everyone to work on one together. This contract might lay out some privacy ground rules for your home. If it's important to you that people knock when entering your room, list that in the agreement. You might also include a rule about sisters or brothers asking to use your things (rather than just taking them). When you have a contract everyone agrees to, have family members sign it.

 **Sample Privacy Contract**

**Mom, Dad, Kala,** and **Phil** agree to respect the privacy of everyone in this family. The purpose of this contract is to remind us that each family member has a need for private time. This contract is also about respecting one another's personal belongings. When we sign this form, we agree to treat one another and other's belongings with respect. We also agree that it's okay to have some time alone. If we want private time, we will let people know in a polite way.

Signed,

*Mom,* Dad, Kala, Phil

# Agreements and Disagreements

You and the people in your family might try very hard to prevent conflicts around hot button issues at home. You may even be really good at working together to resolve many of the disagreements that do come up. But what can you do when you and your parents just can't seem to agree on what to do about a situation? You can work together to come up with a compromise everyone can live with.

For example, maybe you've recently had some disagreements about your allowance. Have a respectful conversation about it and figure out why you disagree. Here's an example of how to bring up the issue:

**You:** "Dad, can we talk about my allowance? Lately, I've been finding that I don't have enough money to get through the week. I think I should get a little more than you're giving me."

**Dad:** "I think your allowance is high enough. Sometimes you don't even do the chores you're supposed to do."

**You:** "I know. If I promise to finish my chores, could you raise my allowance?"

**Dad:** "How do I know you're really going to get them done?"

**You:** "Give me a chance to prove it to you. In two weeks, if I'm not doing better, you can keep the amount of my allowance the same."

**Dad:** "Sounds good. You know, I'd even be willing to give you a little extra money for extra chores."

**You:** "Great! Now, let's put it in writing."

"My parents and I just don't seem to see things the same way. I try to understand them, but it's hard. I wish they listened more to my side of things."
—**Cheryl, 13**

Type up the agreement and print off two copies so each person has a copy. If you put the agreement someplace where you'll see it each day, you'll be more likely to remember what you've said you'll do. It's not enough to simply make a promise, you have to keep it, too.

After you've made the first agreement and stuck to it for a month or so, it will feel like part of your normal routine. Most likely, you'll find that you and your parents have stopped arguing about the issue. At that point, you can decide if you're ready to make a new agreement. Go back to the list of hot buttons (see page 68) to see which one is causing conflict.

Suppose you and your parents have been arguing about how messy your room is. Maybe you're content living with clutter on every surface and a laundry pile a mile high, and they're not. Can both sides agree to give a little, so you can put the argument to rest? Maybe you could come up with an agreement like this:

**You agree to:**

- make your bed every day before school
- empty your trash can at least once a week
- keep clean clothes off the floor

**Your parents agree to:**

- stop criticizing your room
- refrain from reminding you to clean up
- shut the door if they can't stand the clutter

What happens if someone breaks an agreement you've made together? Decide ahead of time what the consequences will be. That way, everyone knows what to expect.

If you're the one who breaks the agreement, admit what you've done and apologize. Taking responsibility for your actions shows maturity. If your mom or dad slips up, talk about it. Explain how you feel about the broken agreement. And be forgiving. After all, parents are human, and they make mistakes, too.

Agreements between you and adults at home can be a good way to come up with solutions to tough situations. Some parents, though, won't be willing to compromise on issues that are important to you. If you think your parents are being unfair about something, talk with another adult you trust about it. Getting someone else's point of view can give you perspective on what's happening. This person might also have ideas about making things better between you and a parent.

 **Family Meetings**

A great time to bring up agreements—and disagreements—is during a family meeting. Here are seven steps you can take to make family meetings work in your home:

1. **Name the time and place.** Decide how often you'll meet (once a month, once a week, whenever a big issue comes up), what time (after dinner, after homework), and where (the kitchen, the living room). You can also set a time limit for the meetings, so they don't drag on too long.

2. **Set up some ground rules.** Important rules include listening respectfully, not interrupting each other, and being sure not to tease, whine, or raise voices.

3. **Decide on a way to begin each meeting.** Start each meeting on a positive note, even if you've gathered to discuss a conflict. Some families begin by letting each person talk about his or her day: What was the best thing that happened? Were there any surprises?

4. **Take turns talking.** Some families pass around a "talking stick" for the person who's speaking to hold. You can use anything for a talking stick. If you'd like, make one for your family. Start with a wooden spoon and add paint or decorations. Whoever is holding the talking stick gets to speak without being interrupted.

5. **Determine how the meetings will be run.** Who will be the leader (or whatever title your family decides to give for this role)? How often will the roles change—every week, every month? Will each family member get an opportunity to lead a meeting?

6. **Decide how to handle the issues that come up.** Does someone need to apologize? Do agreements need to be made? Make an effort to resolve the issues in each meeting. Don't give up!

**7. Come up with a way to end the meetings.** Go for something upbeat. For example, create a fun slogan to end every meeting. Other ideas include having each person say one positive thing about another family member or express one thing they're grateful for.

It's helpful to have a regular time and place to share thoughts, opinions, or misunderstandings—and to talk about solutions. These meetings are a positive step in building a healthy relationship with your family and bringing everyone a little closer.

# Tough Times at Home

Good communication and family meetings can solve or prevent many family problems. But these tools aren't enough for every family situation. Some family problems are too big or serious for those solutions. These problems are the ones everyone hopes to avoid. You or your friends might have parents who fight a lot or have divorced. Maybe a family member has a serious illness or there are money problems. Some people spend time living in foster care because a parent isn't able to take care of them.

During the middle school years, many tweens and teens experience difficult family situations. At these times—whether it's divorce, living in a stepfamily, the absence of a loved one, a move, or the loss of a home—it's natural to feel painful emotions like anger, guilt, or sadness. It's important to remember that these changes to your family aren't your fault.

How you react to tough times or transitions at home will often depend, in part, on how the adults in your life are handling them. While it might be hard to adjust to how things are at first, most difficult situations improve over time or you find better ways to respond to them. When you're upset about a family issue, it's important to talk to your parents about your feelings. It may also be helpful to talk to a friend, especially one who has gone through a similar situation.

**When Home Isn't Safe**

You have a right to feel safe and protected from harm or abuse at home. If you ever feel unsafe, it's important to get help right away. Talk with an adult you can trust. It might be a relative in your extended family (like an aunt, an uncle, or a grandparent), a person at school (such as a teacher, coach, or counselor), or someone in your faith community. You might feel awkward sharing family problems, but keeping problems locked inside you to protect your family's privacy can only lead to further harm. If there's no one you feel you can talk to, call the Boys Town National Hotline (1-800-448-3000). This 24/7 hotline (for boys *and* girls) can connect you with the help you need.

# The Sibling Scene

If you have a brother or sister, you already know that sibling rivalry is a natural fact of life. You might have a sister or brother who tattles on you to get you in trouble with parents or refuses to do a fair share of the chores. Maybe there's a lot of jealousy or teasing that goes on between you. You may be annoyed by a little brother who insists on hanging around when you're with friends, or a younger sister who always invades your privacy. (This can be especially common among siblings who share a room.)

No siblings get along all the time. Sometimes, when you and a sibling argue about who gets to sit in the most comfortable chair, who gets to stay up later, or something else, what you're really in conflict about is attention and love from your parents.

As soon as there were two of you, you and your brother or sister probably started keeping careful records of who got more or less at any given time—without even realizing it. In fact, every time either one of you said, "Mom, no fair that he got more than me!" or "Dad, watch *me* now!" what you were really saying was, "Show me you love me, too!" This is true whether you're the firstborn, a middle child, or the youngest in the family. Everyone with a sibling has, at some point, felt worried about getting a fair share of love and attention.

One thing to remember is that having a brother or sister is like having a special gift. Siblings can be great listeners, advice-givers, and secret-keepers. But only if you have a strong relationship based on love and respect.

Whether your sibling relationship is good or not-so-good, you can do something to improve it. Here are some ideas:

**Every day, do one thing (big or small) to show love for a brother or sister.** Offer a kind word, a compliment, or some help with a chore or homework.

**Once a week, spend time together playing a game both of you like.** This is a healthy way to compete with each other—and have fun at the same time.

**Confide in each other.** You may get along well with your parents, but perhaps they don't always understand the things that are important to someone your age. It helps to talk to a sister or brother. Remember, though, secrets need to be kept private. If you tell each other's secrets, you won't be able to trust each other again. (An exception to this rule is if you're worried about your sibling, and you need to go to a parent for help.)

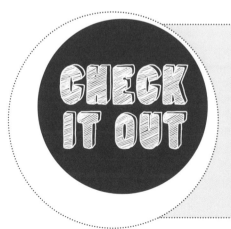

**Families Change**
**www.familieschange.ca**
Visit this website for advice on how to deal with transitions that can affect families, including divorce and living in a stepfamily.

**Nineline**
**www.nineline.org**
This website has information that can be helpful for dealing with tough times at home.

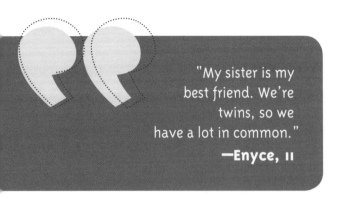

"My sister is my best friend. We're twins, so we have a lot in common."

**—Enyce, 11**

**Ask for advice and give it in return.** This is one of the nicest things siblings can do for each other—especially since you know and understand each other so well!

**If you have younger sisters or brothers, think of ways they can help you.** Little kids love to be of help and feel included. If you want help with a chore, ask your younger brother or sister to pitch in. If you've misplaced something, chances are your younger sibling can find it by crawling under the bed or looking in other places you might not think of. Come up with other creative ways to get a sibling's help—and remember to lend a hand in return.

**If you have older sisters or brothers, think of ways they can help you.** Your older siblings probably know a little bit more about life since they've lived longer than you. Talk to them about mistakes they've made or lessons they've learned. Find out what middle school was like for them.

**Make each other laugh.** Tell each other jokes and riddles. Watch a funny movie together. Play a game of charades. Practice your best imitations in front of each other. Whatever gets you laughing!

# Staying Close to Your Family

Watch this. It's the best part!

Family is an important part of life. The people who love you can be a strong source of support, now and into adulthood. But that doesn't mean relationships with parents, siblings, and other family members are always easy. If you're struggling to connect with loved ones, try to figure out what's making things difficult. Set up a family meeting, so all members can express their points of view. Then take steps to solve the issues that come up.

Families can strengthen their connections in other ways, too. If you want to build family togetherness, here are seven tips to try:

1. **Have a family night.** You can have family night once a week, once a month, or whenever you want. Choose a night and mark it on the calendar so everyone remembers. That can be your evening to cook a meal together, watch a DVD, attend a sporting event, play a board game, or do anything else your family enjoys.

2. **Volunteer together.** Volunteering your time and energy will help you feel good about yourselves and the people (or animals) you're helping. Plus, this is a great way to spend time together! You can serve food at a soup kitchen, clean up litter in your community, or walk dogs at a local animal shelter. Explore volunteering options that are available within your community or through your place of worship.

3. **Put your creativity to work—as a team.** Have you ever considered making your own electronic family newsletter? Family members can contribute their unique talents—creating articles, cartoons, editorials, movie reviews, an advice column, or interviews on the computer. Another idea is to create a digital photo album together, so you can relive memories while creating a lasting project everyone can enjoy.

4. **Plan a family vacation.** A vacation doesn't have to be far away or expensive to be fun. How about camping? Or taking a long weekend to explore sights in your community or state? Or what about a vacation in your own home? If you'd like to travel during vacation, perhaps everyone in the family can work together to save extra money.

5. **Create new family traditions.** How does your family celebrate Thanksgiving? Valentine's Day? The New Year? What about Christmas, Hanukkah, Kwanzaa, Ramadan, or other religious occasions? Each family observes holidays in its own unique way, and these events can be a special time of celebration and family closeness. Think about your family's traditions: do you honor them each year? Find new ways to personalize the holidays, while maintaining your old traditions. For example,

you might create one-of-a-kind decorations or give each other handmade gifts.

6. **Make a family scrapbook.** Help everyone remember the interesting things that happened during a holiday, a summer, or even a whole year by creating a family scrapbook. You'll need a scrapbook, glue, and mementos from each family member, such as photos, ticket stubs, or favorite sayings. Arrange the items on each page in an artistic way and add some decorations.

7. **Keep in touch with relatives.** Is there one person in your family who sends all the birthday and holiday cards to relatives? Why not give that person a hand? You can also keep in touch with relatives on your own by emailing them and attaching digital photos. A fun family project is to make a DVD to mail to faraway family members. Be sure to keep a copy for your home.

## A Closing Thought...

The middle school years are a time when you're becoming more independent, but your family is still an important connection for you. In a way, you're kind of like a boat going out to sea: there's plenty of fun and adventure ahead, but isn't it a little bit comforting to know that, not too far in the distance, there's a shore you can head to when the seas get rough?

Family life isn't always smooth sailing, as you probably know. But a strong family relationship can be one of your greatest sources of support—now and always.

# Find, Make, and Keep Friends

Friendships are very important during the middle school years. You might already spend a lot of time hanging out with friends, texting, playing video games, or participating in sports and other activities. These fun experiences can really strengthen friendships. But the middle school social scene also has challenges. Starting at another school might mean a lot of new faces in class and at lunch. Friends sometimes abandon one another to hang out with a more "popular" crowd. Cliques often form and exclude or tease nonmembers. These situations can all be tough to deal with, but **Survival Tip #5** can help. It's all about finding, making, and keeping good friends—skills that can help you now and in the future. You'll also find info on dating, another part of middle school life you may be wondering about.

# What's Friendship All About?

When you were younger, you probably made friends with the people in your neighborhood. But now you're older, and many things in your life have changed. You have new interests and activities, and more freedom to do what you like to do. At school, you may change rooms to attend different classes, instead of staying in the same room all day long. You're probably meeting more people now, which gives you lots of opportunities to make friends.

## Making Friends

Making friends is all about getting to know new people. If you're naturally kind of shy, you may find it harder to make friends. But, you'll find that building friendships can get easier with practice. And one simple piece of advice can take you a long way: Be yourself. You don't need to put on an act to get people interested in you or make them think you're popular. Real friends like you for who you are.

> "I have kept most of my friends from elementary school, but I see a lot of new groups in school. Sometimes the groups change one day to the next day."
> **—Amir, 12**

> "Before, everyone played together in a big group. But now, people hang out and some kids don't want to hang out with other kids so you have to think about your friendships more."
> **—Matthew, 11**

> "Making new friends in middle school isn't that hard. You just start talking to people in class or at your locker or on your team and then you become friends. But you have to have something in common to stay friends."
> **—Shana, 13**

**Boy Scouts of America**
**www.scouting.org**
Check out this program for guys to get involved in camping trips, outdoor adventures, and service projects in the community.

**Girl Scouts of the U.S.A.**
**www.girlscouts.org**
Activities available from this organization for girls explore topics ranging from sports to science and service to careers.

**Get out and about.** A friend isn't going to magically show up at your door! Find out what's going on in your neighborhood and community. Is there a sports team you can join? A local recreation center you can check out? Maybe a community-sponsored club? What do people nearby do for fun?

**Join in at school.** Participating in an after-school activity is a great way to get to know people. What are your interests—drama, writing, art, athletics, community service, computers, music? Plenty of activities are available in middle school. Figure out what you like to do, and then get involved.

**Be friendly at school.** You may be surprised at how quickly other people respond to a smile or friendly hello. To break the ice, you could ask someone for the homework assignment or say something about a teacher or class. After the other person responds, try to get a conversation going. Ask questions and act interested. Most people like to talk about themselves and appreciate it when someone listens.

How can you tell if someone is a potential friend? You'll feel a connection to the person. Maybe you have a lot in common—you like the same jokes or activities. Sometimes you and your friend might be very different—one of you may be more athletic, and the other more social. But you admire each other's positive qualities, and together, you complement each other.

If there's someone at school you're interested in getting to know, invite that person to do something fun. Shoot some hoops, go for a bike ride, or just sit together at lunch. Have a party and invite people you'd like to get to know better. Soon enough, you'll receive invitations in return.

 ## Fun Things to Do with Friends

What do you like to do with your friends? Maybe you spend a lot of time hanging out, using the computer, playing video games, or just texting. Want some new ideas for fun things to do? Here are a few to try:

- Learn a new sport or musical instrument together. You could start a band.

- Join an after-school club together or start a club your school or town doesn't have.

- Volunteer on a project that helps your community.

- Plan an outdoor party with different games and lots of food.

- Start a business together. You could wash cars, do lawn work, make crafts to sell, create greeting cards, take care of people's pets, or find other ways to earn money.

- Start a book club. Choose a book to start with and see that everyone in the club gets a copy from the library or bookstore. Meet to talk about what you've read.

- Join a new club or youth group, such as the Girl Scouts, Boy Scouts, or Boys and Girls Clubs.

# Being a Good Friend

Are you a good friend? And how can you tell? Ask yourself if you're . . .

**Dependable:** Do you call when you say you will? Are you on time when you and your friends make plans? Do you keep secrets a secret? Are you there when your friends need help or advice?

**Loyal:** Can your friends rely on you to stick up for them? Do you make them a priority in your life?

**Supportive:** Do you cheer on your friends in every effort? Do you listen? Do you point out your friends' positive qualities? Are you kind and helpful?

**Considerate:** Do you take into account your friends' feelings? Do you make an effort to understand their points of view?

**Respectful:** Do you treat your friends the way you would like to be treated? Do you appreciate your friends' unique qualities?

If you answered yes to all of these questions, *congratulations!* You're a good friend, and that's an excellent quality. Maybe you answered yes to many but not all of the questions. Are you still a good friend? Sure, but you can become an even better one.

Decide where you need to improve. Can you call your friend more often? Make an effort to listen? Compliment your friend more? Consider your friend's feelings? Be

> "The best friend to have is one who cares about you and will stand by your side when something happens to you."
> **—Chris, 13**

> "A friend is someone who's kind, lets you talk, stands up for you—and shares lunch with you when you've forgotten yours."
> **—Brianna, 12**

> "A good friend is someone you can trust 100%."
> **—Jorge, 12**

more respectful? Make an effort to do one thing (or more) each week to be a better friend.

What if a friend of yours is the one who needs to work on his or her friendship skills? It may not be easy telling your friend how you feel, but talking can help. Here's what to do:

**Agree on a good time to talk.** Find a private place where you won't have to worry about other people listening in.

**Be honest and direct.** Don't accuse your friend of anything; just calmly explain how you feel.

**Listen to your friend.** If you want your friend to hear what you have to say, make sure you're doing your part by listening.

# When You're Not Getting Along

Friendships have highs and lows. Sometimes you and a friend may be so close that you're almost like family. At other times, the two of you may feel so angry with each other that you wonder why you ever became friends in the first place. How do you keep your friendship strong when you're not getting along? Try conflict resolution.

**1. Decide what the problem really is.** Sometimes the fight has gotten so big that the people involved can't even remember what the original problem was. Or maybe the fight is hiding the real problem. For example:

Renee is hurt and angry that her friend, Ayesha, has been spending a lot of time with a new girl at school. Renee doesn't want to admit how she really feels, so instead she tells Ayesha not to bother coming over Friday night even though they had plans. When Ayesha asks her why she shouldn't come over, Renee says she just changed her mind. Now Ayesha's hurt and angry, too.

Figuring out the real problem means both sides have to be very honest about their feelings.

**2. Come up with solutions.** Think of as many as possible and make a long list of ideas.

**3. Choose the solution that both sides agree is best.** What would each person like to see happen? Is there an obvious solution?

"Arguments are going to happen between friends, but don't let them make you forget why you like each other."
—**Jonathon, 12**

If not, is there a way to compromise? The goal here is to find a win/win solution, meaning something positive happens for both people involved. For example, consider what solutions might work in the following situation:

Evan has been taking guitar lessons, and his music teacher suggested that he join the school band. Evan decides to give band a try, but his best friend, Mike, gets mad because Evan now has band practice on Thursdays after school. That was the day Evan always came to Mike's home to hang out. Evan feels guilty, but he's also mad that Mike is acting so selfish.

Possible solutions might include:

- Evan quits the band and continues to go to Mike's house: this is good for Mike, but Evan is missing out on a chance to play in the band.

- Mike stays home alone on Thursday afternoons, while Evan's at band: this allows Evan to stay in the band, but Mike is bored on Thursday afternoons.

- Evan and Mike stay angry with each other and end their friendship: both guys lose a friend because neither was willing to compromise.

- Evan stays in the band, and Mike signs up for chess club, which meets on Thursday afternoons. The boys decide to get together on Wednesdays instead: win/win!

Now the goal is to agree to act on the solution that works best for both sides.

**4. Apologize.** Each person should apologize—and mean it. Forgive one another and put the conflict to rest.

**5. Use a little humor.** There's nothing like laughter to loosen up a tense situation. After a serious conversation, it helps to tell a joke or remind each other of a time when you did something really weird or goofy. It's hard to stay angry when you're laughing!

# Friendship Pitfalls

You can't help feeling jealous sometimes. Maybe your best friend gets A's in all her classes but barely studies. Another friend may be very sure of himself and always know what to say to get laughs from the crowd. You, on the other hand, might struggle for B's at school and stay quiet in social situations because you're sure you'll say something dumb. Maybe you don't want to let these things make you jealous, but you can't help it. So what to do?

Accept that it's normal to feel jealous sometimes. Just don't let jealousy eat away at you and make you hard to be around. Instead, think of the positive things you've accomplished. Maybe you recently made the volleyball team, got a good grade on an assignment, or taught your little sister how to skateboard. Thinking of your pluses can protect you from feeling jealous.

Remember, too, that if something good happens to your friend, it's a positive thing. Feeling happy for your friend is a way to show support. If you can't seem to get over your jealousy, ask yourself what's going on. Does your friend have something you want? If so, is there a way you can get the same thing? Instead of putting energy into feeling envious, set a goal for yourself and take steps to reach it. This way, you're focusing on yourself (instead of your friend) and using positive thinking to your advantage.

Sometimes jealousy is low self-esteem in disguise. Maybe you feel that you aren't as smart, good-looking, organized, athletic, outgoing, or confident as your friend. Instead of finding ways you don't measure up, think of what makes you stand out. What's unique about you? What are your positive traits? What makes you fun to be with? Take a look at pages 27–29 for more on feeling good about yourself.

Jealousy isn't the only friendship "monster" to look out for: betrayal is a big one, too. A betrayal is a break in trust, such as lying or saying something negative behind a friend's back. Betrayals cause anger and hurt feelings—and can bust up even the strongest friendships.

What if you've betrayed a friend: is there any way to repair the damage? Start by admitting what you've done and saying you're sorry. Apologizing shows that you care and you want to make up. A good friend will probably forgive you if your apology is sincere. Make a promise never to betray your friend again— and keep that promise.

"One of my friends seems to have everything. Sometimes I wish I could trade places with her."

—Jhumpa, 11

If a friend has betrayed you, talk about what happened. Let your friend know how you feel. If your friend apologizes, try to put the hurt behind you. Any friendship worth having is usually worth saving, too.

# When Friendships End

While friendships are often worth saving, not all of them are necessarily meant to last forever. People change, and so do relationships. Sometimes friends grow apart and can't find a way to reconnect. At other times, conflicts between friends aren't resolved and the friendship ends. If you've ever lost a friend, you know it can hurt. One way to feel better is to stay involved in activities at home and at school.

At some point, you may be the one who has to end a friendship. A friend may be doing things that make you uncomfortable—like taking drugs or shoplifting. Or a friend may be too demanding and expect you not to have any other friends. Ending a friendship is hard. You don't want to hurt the person, so what can you do?

Before ending it, decide whether fixing the friendship is possible. Sometimes an honest conversation can save a friendship. On the other hand, maybe you've already tried talking things over and there's no hope for the friendship. If this is the case, you can try two different ways of ending it:

**#1. Be honest and tell the person you want to stop being friends.** This option may be more difficult, but it's the recommended one. When you're honest, the other person knows where you stand. He or she isn't left hanging on to a friendship that no longer exists.

Here are some examples of what you might say:

- "I know we've been friends for a long time, but I don't feel as close to you anymore. Do you feel the same way?"

- "We were close last year, but this year I have new activities, and you have different interests and new friends. Maybe we don't have time for each other right now."

- "I feel like you're into things that aren't right for me, so I can't hang around with you anymore."

**#2. You can end the friendship gradually by getting involved in activities that your friend isn't into.** This option may seem easier, but it doesn't make it as clear to the other person that you don't want to be friends. In fact, it may take longer for the friendship to dissolve. But some people feel more comfortable letting a friendship fade instead of ending it all at once. Choose the option that's right for you.

## Online Friends and Privacy

Most middle schoolers enjoy connecting with friends online at social sites and by playing video games together. Many also enjoy texting back and forth on cell phones. All of these activities can be a lot of fun, but they can also take up a lot of time. You may have to balance the time you spend in the virtual world with the time you spend in the real world. It's also good to keep in mind some important ground rules:

**Always protect personal information.** You can make a lot of "friends" online, but giving out information about yourself (like your full name, address, phone number, school address, and sports teams) exposes you to the entire world. The same is true when you are in a virtual world or playing online games. Create a screen name that doesn't give out information about you (like your age, real name, or hometown). Also avoid filling out entry forms or Web pages without permission from parents. These forms are often nothing more than phony contests meant to gather personal data.

If you have a profile on a social media site, it's important to pay attention to the privacy settings. Make your profile private or for people on your friends list who you already know. Also, if you use a cell phone that lets friends know where you are, make sure that information is available to only those you really trust. Remember that it's important to avoid sharing personal information about your friends, too.

**Be careful posting images online.** Once you have placed your picture on a public website, you can *never* delete it from all of the places it may wind up. Photos can also easily be changed in ways that can hurt your reputation, so it's important to be careful. Get permission from parents

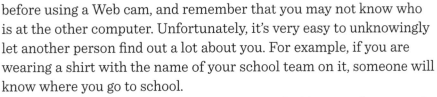

"Being online with my friends is another way to hang out, but really we have more fun in person."
**—Al, 12**

before using a Web cam, and remember that you may not know who is at the other computer. Unfortunately, it's very easy to unknowingly let another person find out a lot about you. For example, if you are wearing a shirt with the name of your school team on it, someone will know where you go to school.

With cameras in a lot of cell phones, handheld game players, and other electronic devices, it's easy for people to take, send, and post online photos and videos of you. Ask friends to respect your wish not to have images of you floating all over cyberspace.

**Never share passwords.** Another important thing to remember is to avoid sharing passwords—even with friends. It may seem okay when you're really close, but if your relationship changes, your former friend could use a password and information about you in ways you won't like. A lot of damage can be done to a person's reputation in a short amount of time.

**Be on the lookout for cyberbullying.** Saying and posting untrue and nasty things and photos of people is a very big problem, including in middle schools. Maybe you or someone you know has been affected by others posting false information online or spreading rumors by text. This type of bullying is extremely hurtful and has even led to people committing suicide. That's why it's important never to bully or put people down online or in text messages. If you are ever the victim of cyberbullying, tell an adult at home or school right away.

**Be aware of suspicious behavior and email.** Be cautious if a new online friend wants to meet you in person or asks you a lot of personal questions. Tell an adult right away, especially if someone harasses you online or wants to talk about sex. Also know that emails and files people send can contain viruses that harm computers. Don't open email messages or files from people you don't know.

**Talk with parents.** Ask the adults at home what they expect from you online. If you're uncertain of what their expectations are for you, or if how you spend your time online causes disagreements, consider creating an agreement (see page 73) with them about what is and is not okay. You could also read and talk about this section together.

Also, think about this: When you are online or texting, you aren't really "there" with other people. Don't miss out on spending time in the real world with family and friends.

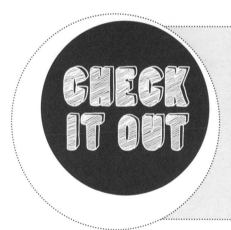

**Internet Safety Site**
**www.netsmartz.org**
Visit this site for information on how to have fun online without putting yourself at risk.

**NS Teens**
**www.nsteens.org**
Videos, games, comics, and real-life stories make this an entertaining site to learn about cyber safety.

# Tough Stuff

Where do I fit in here?

Mostly middle school can be great, but not always. Being the new kid, cliques, bullies, peer pressure . . . they're facts of middle school life. These situations are tough—but not impossible—to deal with.

For example, what if you come home from school one day and find out the move your parents have been considering is actually going to happen? Suddenly you'll be going to a new home and school—and that means you'll be the new kid. Even if you're looking forward to the move, you'll need courage to make new friends.

Most likely, you won't find a welcoming committee knocking on your door. But some of the people at school will probably make an effort to get to know you. If some seem friendly, see if you can sit with them at lunch, and ask one of them to show you around school or introduce you to other people. Find out if there are other new people—they'll probably be happy to meet another person who's new, too. Be sure to join some school activities where you'll find people—and potential friends—who share your interests and talents.

If you're unsure of how to approach people, practice introducing yourself and getting a conversation going. You don't have to have an entire comedy routine ready—just think about ways to say, "Hi, I'm _____ (your name)."

When you talk to new people, ask questions and really listen to their answers. Most people are attracted to a good listener. (Besides, you'll have plenty of opportunities to talk about yourself later in the friendship.)

After you have a new group of friends, you'll feel more comfortable. You'll have people to sit with at lunch, talk to between classes, and spend time with after school and on weekends. All of this will help you feel more at home.

## The Ins and Outs of Middle School

Every school has groups. The people who hang out together often share the same interests—sports, music, academics, and so on. Even in elementary school, you probably knew which groups were considered more popular. But in elementary school, popularity probably wasn't as important.

In middle school, however, groups often start to get labeled. Most people know which groups are "in," or "out," or somewhere in-between. Unfortunately, the labels become a way to define who people are and where they weigh in on the popularity scale.

Many tweens and teens don't care which group they're in, as long as they have good friends to hang around with. They know that labels don't mean much. But some people will do almost anything to be accepted by the "in" group or clique. They copy the group's clothing and language in an effort to be accepted. But often, the harder they try to fit in and achieve popularity, the more desperate they seem to others.

Have you ever tried to change your image to fit in with a group or become more popular? If you have, you're not alone. Some tweens and teens look forward to each new school year as a chance to finally get in with the "popular" group.

The real secret to popularity is being yourself. You may have heard this before—that's because it's the truth. Instead of changing your image, work on getting comfortable with yourself. Do the sports or activities you like—not whichever ones are considered "cool." Wear clothes that you feel good in and are comfortable—not ones that match the styles of a certain group. Don't assume you have to be the class clown or downplay your smarts to be accepted. Act confident, even if you don't always feel very confident.

"Popularity isn't really important. It's an extra—something you can live without."
—Donna, 13

"When I first got to middle school, I really wanted to be popular. But, by eighth grade, I realized having a group of good friends was much more important."
—Marcus, 14

"I think in middle school you can get pressured to do things you know aren't the right things to do. You need friends that share your values and keep you on a good path."
—Maya, 12

Most of all, be aware that popularity isn't a measure of your worth as a person. If you like who you are, it will show. People who feel good about themselves make other people feel good about themselves—and that makes them fun to be around!

## Handling Peer Pressure

Peer pressure gets a lot stronger in middle school. When friends or people at school try to convince you to do something you really don't want to do, you're feeling peer pressure. You may be pressured about

## FAST FACT

If you sometimes feel the urge to give in to peer pressure, you're not alone. Many experts believe that the middle school years are the time when pressure to fit in is strongest. The good news? Once everyone gets to high school, peer pressure often has less of an effect. By then, people have a stronger sense of who they want to be, which can make it a lot easier to stand up to others. When you stand up to peer pressure today, you're showing maturity beyond your years. Not a bad thing at all!

some not-so-serious things—like the clothes you wear or the club you join at school, the shows you watch on TV, or the activities you do after school. But sometimes, you may feel pressured about very serious activities—like drinking alcohol, bullying another person, using other drugs, smoking cigarettes, writing graffiti, or shoplifting. These are negative risky behaviors. What should you do if other people push you to take negative risks?

Sometimes, you may be tempted to do what the other people want you to do just so they'll leave you alone. Before acting, take a deep breath and try to see the situation clearly. Are all of your friends pressuring you, or just one or a few? If only one or two are trying to make you do something you don't want to do, get your other friends to take your side and reverse the pressure. You may feel more secure making a stand if other people are behind you.

On the other hand, you may have to face up to the pressure alone. Standing up for yourself takes courage. You may feel that saying no to the crowd will mean losing face or losing friends.

Before deciding what to do, consider what's at stake. What might the consequences of your actions be? Are you taking a chance with your health, safety, or future? If you're worried about what the others will think of you if you say no, ask yourself how much their opinion really matters to you. What will taking the risk do to your opinion of yourself? Think through your options before making a choice.

How do you say no and mean it? How do you ensure that people will listen to you and respect your decision? Practice being assertive, so you can say no with conviction. "Um, well, I don't think so, okay?" doesn't sound like you mean it. When you're alone, rehearse what you'll say and how you'll say it. Here are some tips:

**Show a sense of humor.** Make a joke or say something funny. For example, if a friend pressures you to smoke, reply, "My parents would ground me for life" or "Smoking stunts your growth and I want to make the basketball team."

**Use a firm no.** You don't have to shout it—just say it assertively. Try "No thanks" or "No, I'm not into that." The more you practice, the easier it will be to respond politely but firmly.

**Have a ready excuse.** Some to try are, "My coach would kill me" or "I'm really late—gotta run!" or "I'll be really sick and throw up." (Then remove yourself from the situation.)

Some people confuse assertiveness and aggressiveness. If you're assertive, you stick up for yourself. You respect yourself and your decisions, and you give honest opinions to your friends. But you don't put other people down. You don't bully others into thinking like you or doing things your way. Those actions are what an aggressive person does. Being aggressive makes other people feel uncomfortable around you. Being assertive earns you their respect.

If you're not used to being assertive, set aside the next couple of weeks to practice your assertiveness skills. Rehearse in front of the mirror, or ask a family member to role-play with you (the family member would pretend to pressure you, so you could practice saying no). Keep at it until sticking up for yourself comes more naturally.

"I don't do anything that doesn't feel right for me—end of story. My friends have to respect that."
**—Alcides, 13**

# Coping with Cliques

There's nothing wrong with belonging to a group of friends. Having a support system at school is important. But when groups of friends close themselves off to others, they become cliques. Some cliques leave others out or make them feel inferior. These kinds of cliques think of themselves as "better" or more "special." Some clique members may convince others that the clique is very desirable, just because it won't let them in.

Not all people in cliques realize how they treat others. They may not even be aware that they're leaving some people out or making them feel unwelcome. This is one reason why being part of a clique can be so confusing. It can also be pretty hard to tell the difference between a group of friends and a clique, so here are some hints for understanding the difference:

**Friends:** include people
**Cliques:** exclude people

**Friends:** are loyal to each other
**Cliques:** have only each other

**Friends:** like each other and people outside the group
**Cliques:** look down on others

**Friends:** encourage individuality
**Cliques:** want each member to be the same

**Friends:** enjoy doing things together and apart
**Cliques:** are hardly ever seen without each other

What happens if you're part of a clique? Ask yourself if that's where you want to be. Often, membership in a clique can make you feel accepted and safe . . . at first. But after a while, you may realize that certain people in the clique act like they're in control. You may have to follow rules about how to dress, talk, and act. This is where peer pressure comes in.

How important is it for you to belong to this clique? Are you doing things you don't feel right about just to make the other clique members think you're cool? If the people you once thought of as friends are now making you miserable, it may be time to break out of the clique. You can find other friends at school or in your community. For tips on making new friends, see pages 85–87.

You don't have to trade your independence for clique dependence. It's up to you to decide which friendships are right for you—and which ones you're better off without.

**CHECK IT OUT**

**Above the Influence**
**www.abovetheinfluence.com**
This website features tips for surviving the social scene at school without compromising who you are.

**Teaching Tolerance—Mix It Up**
**www.teachingtolerance/mixitup**
Go here to learn how your school can hold a Mix It Up event. These special days encourage students to move beyond their usual social groups to connect with new people at school.

## Dealing with Bullying

Bullies—every school and neighborhood has them. You probably know certain people in your school who do a lot of bullying. They may be male or female, smart or not-so-smart, popular or unpopular. Hurting or picking on other people gives them a feeling of power and protection.

You should know that almost every middle school kid feels like he or she has been the target of bullying at one time or another. The problem seems to be worst in middle school and then starts to fade in high school. Why? Maybe in middle school being popular is so important that some people will do anything, including bully others, to get there. That probably doesn't make you feel a whole lot better if you are the target of someone who is bullying you.

Bullying can be done in many ways. Some people like to play mind games. They'll talk behind your back, get other people to make fun of you, and even cause your friends to ignore you. You may not have any idea why you're the target. Some people who act like bullies may be shocked if you told them that's how they were acting. They may think their behavior is normal or funny or the best way to be popular. Sometimes they do what they do because they've learned these behaviors from a parent or another adult. Research shows that some bullies have been mistreated, so they bully others to feel stronger and more in control. Or they may not know any other way to act.

If someone bullies you, it can be hard to make the person stop. Here are some things you can do:

**Get your friends to support you.** It's harder to pick on someone who's surrounded by friends.

**Avoid the bully.** Don't be alone in the school hallways, bathrooms, or other places where the person might find you.

**Walk or run away from the person.** Get to a safe place as quickly as possible.

**Talk to an adult.** Go to a parent, teacher, principal, bus driver, or another adult for help. If the person does not take you seriously, tell another adult. Keep reporting the bullying until someone listens to you.

**Tell the person firmly and assertively to stop bothering you.** You can say, "I don't like the way you're treating me. I'll report you if you keep this up."

**Report bullying that takes place online or by cell phone.** If someone is hurting you or your reputation via email, online posts, text messages, or other electronic messages, tell an adult right away.

You have to know many ways to deal with bullying because no one way is necessarily best. For example, avoiding the person may be impossible if you ride on the same bus. In some cases, a bully may stop the behavior for a while, only to start up again.

You may need to try new ways to get the person off your back. Don't give up! No one has a right to pick on you, tease you, threaten you, or cause you any other kind of harm.

If you're the one doing the bullying, it's time to make a change. Hurting people isn't a way to make yourself feel better or more popular. When you make fun of people, freeze them out, write or say nasty things about them, you are acting like a bully. Think about why you're acting this way. Talk to an adult you trust for help stopping what you are doing.

At some schools, bullies get away with their behavior for way too long. Bullying can be severe, and victims may think there's no way out. Even if others are aware of what's going on, they may be afraid to speak up. Some very tragic things can happen when bullying goes unreported. Afterward, people often wish they had said or done something to make the bullying stop.

Bullying wouldn't be so easy to do if people didn't give in to it. If you know someone is being bullied, it's important to act. If you feel safe, you can stand up for the person who is being mistreated. If you are worried for your safety, get an adult for help right away.

If bullying is a problem at your school, you can help put a stop to it. Talk to your friends about times they were bullied and ask how they handled it. Find out what they learned and what advice they'd give others targeted by bullying. You can also talk to your friends about staying together and sticking up for one another. A group of good friends—even a group of just two or three—can be your best bully-proofing strategy.

You might work with teachers and other adults at school to find ways to end bullying, too. Remember to also tell your parents about bullying, including incidents that might occur in your neighborhood. This is really important even if it is very hard to do. Some kids may feel like tattletales or think their parents won't understand. But bullying is something you have to talk about with an adult you trust.

"Every day you see kids acting mean—they think mean is normal. It isn't, but it's hard to convince them of that!"
—**Maggie, 13**

*Bullies Are a Pain in the Brain*
by Trevor Romain. If you're picked on, pushed around, threatened, or teased, this book is for you. Find out what makes bullies tick, and learn how to bully-proof yourself.

**Stop Bullying Now**
**www.stopbullyingnow.hrsa.gov/kids**
Visit this site for tips and games on bullying prevention as well as webisodes featuring cool characters overcoming challenges at school.

## Violence in School

You may have heard stories of kids who brought weapons to school and hurt or killed other students or teachers. Maybe you have experienced violence in your own school. Sometimes bullying is at the root of the violence.

In many cases, people who feel rejected, lonely, or on the outside blame the rest of the school for their feelings. They get angry and have no way to let the anger out safely. So they reach for a gun and hurt innocent people and themselves. In some cases, a student who acts out in violence is popular, and no one can explain his or her actions. Always, though, people at school later remember signs that their classmate was having problems.

If you hear someone talking about blowing up the school or shooting people, don't assume it won't happen or treat the words as a joke. Tell an adult right away if you hear somebody making a threat against other students, teachers, or school officials. If you know that another student at school has a gun or another weapon, tell a school official immediately—even if the person you're reporting is a friend. In many cases of school violence, students later admitted they'd heard people making threats but hadn't taken them seriously.

School should be a safe place—not a place you're afraid to go. You can help make your school more secure. Here are some ideas:

- Start by getting together a group of people who are committed to the idea of making your school a safer place.
- Invite a teacher or school official to work with you.
- Publicize your efforts through posters or other outlets such as the school newspaper, radio station, or website.
- Help plan a school assembly or program on school safety.
- Ask a teacher to help you involve community groups, such as law enforcement officials, the PTA, or youth organizations.

# Crushes, Flirting, Dating, and More

Sometime soon, if not already, you'll discover you're interested in certain people on more than just a friendship level. Feelings of attraction are a normal part of growing up. As your body changes, your emotions do, too. In fact, during the next couple of years, you may find that you're very emotional—up one minute, down the next—and some of these feelings are tied to love.

Often, the first romantic feeling you have is a crush. Crushes are intense, but usually don't last long. You can have a crush on someone your own age, but many people also have crushes on someone older—maybe an older teen, a neighbor, a teacher, or even someone they don't know at all, like a celebrity or an athlete. You can get a crush on someone of the opposite sex, or someone who's the same sex as you. No matter who the crush is on, the emotions are very strong. Yet, crushes aren't true relationships because they're so one-sided. Often, the person you have a crush on isn't even aware of how you feel. Crushes are practice, in a way, for real love.

What's real love? It's a feeling that's hard to describe and understand because it shows itself in many ways. The love you have for your mom or dad, for example, isn't the same type you feel for a close friend. And that kind of affection is different from how you might feel toward a boy or girl you're interested in. In fact, you may like someone in a romantic way, but this doesn't mean you're in love.

You probably see lots of romantic scenes in media and may think you should have a love life that resembles what you see on the big or small screen. But, the truth is, real relationships are hardly ever so passion-filled.

If you're definitely interested in someone, how do you let that person know? One way is to flirt. Some people are naturals at flirting, but most need practice. Flirting might include looking at the person, smiling, giving compliments, and laughing at his or her jokes. Flirting also includes being genuinely interested in what the person is saying, listening carefully, and giving him or her your undivided attention.

You have probably noticed that some people seem to flirt with just about everybody. They might flirt a lot to get attention or be noticed. But sometimes, this behavior sends the wrong signals. Being a flirt might make someone think you're interested when you really aren't. Once you know the power of flirting, use it with care.

Knowing the difference between innocent flirting and unwanted attention is important. Getting noticed by a boy or girl can be flattering. But sometimes, this type of attention isn't appreciated and can take a dangerous turn toward harassment. When a person bothers you in a sexual kind of way, it's called sexual harassment. Here are some examples:

- A boy snaps a girl's bra strap and makes rude comments about her body.
- A girl whistles at a boy every time he passes her in the hallway.
- Whenever two boys sit behind a girl on the bus, they loudly tell jokes or stories about sex.
- Two girls constantly make comments about the physical characteristics of the boys in their classes.
- A girl posts embarrassing cell phone photos of her "friend" on the Internet.
- In the gym locker room, one boy constantly tries to snap another boy with a towel.

It isn't always easy to recognize sexual harassment or how serious it can be. Some people think their comments or behavior are all in fun or are a kind of flirting. They may even think they're giving the victim a compliment. If you're getting attention that makes you feel uncomfortable or unsafe, you could be experiencing sexual harassment. Don't assume the harasser is only trying to be funny or flirtatious.

No one should ever have to put up with harassment—at school, online, or anywhere else. If someone harasses you, you can say something like, "Stop making those comments" or "I don't like to hear that type of thing." However, in some cases, you may not be able to put a stop to the harassment on your own. You can get help from an adult (a parent, school counselor, teacher, or school official), including if you get a harassing text or are targeted online. You deserve better than to be harassed.

# Dating Dilemmas

What happens if you like somebody, you flirt a little, and the other person responds positively to the attention? Now what do you do?

At some middle schools, students talk about "going with" or "going out with" someone, or "dating." These terms usually mean a boy and girl are in some kind of relationship. They may sit together at lunch, text each other, "friend" each other online, spend time together after school, dance together at school events, or hang out with each other on the weekends—or they may never go out anywhere alone. These relationships may last a day, a week, or a month (sometimes longer).

During the middle school years, you may feel ready to be in a relationship—or not. There's no "right" age to start getting interested in romance. Have you talked about these issues with your mom or dad? Some parents don't allow dating until age fifteen or older. Depending on your cultural background, family adults may be very strict about this kind of thing. They may not want you to go to dances, parties, or other social events that involve both girls and boys.

If you're allowed to date and you want to explore relationships, the easiest way to start is in a group. On group dates, guys and girls hang out together, and there isn't as much pressure to be a couple. The advantage of group settings is you get to know people as friends first. And you may even decide that these friendships are more important to you than dating right now.

If you've already started dating, be careful about going out with someone older. Being with someone older may seem exciting, but you may feel pressured to get physical in ways you're not ready for. Also, if you think about it, doesn't it seem inappropriate for someone much older than you to be interested in someone your age? It definitely is! Most people aren't emotionally ready to get serious about another person during the middle school years. Even if you and the boy or girl you're seeing are the same age, you may have different expectations about how far to go. The fact is, if someone truly cares about you, that person shouldn't try to make you do things you don't want to do.

At this stage of your life, you probably have a lot of questions about sex. Your mom or dad may already have talked to you about it, and maybe you've learned about the topic at school. You might have looked at books or websites to get more information. Most likely, some of your friends and classmates are confused about sex, too. Sometimes, tweens and teens try to seem sophisticated and knowledgeable about sex, when they actually aren't. You may hear "facts" that aren't true, which can confuse you more.

Instead of relying on friends and other people your own age for information about sex, go to an adult you trust. Talking to a parent or other adult about touchy subjects may feel uncomfortable at first—for both of you! But once you get over the initial embarrassment, discussing sex becomes easier. Being open about the subject can help you now and as you face more decisions in the years ahead.

What if you don't feel ready for all this relationship stuff and you're not interested in dating right now? You may be afraid others will think you're immature if you don't want a boyfriend or girlfriend, but it's totally normal to wait a while before getting involved in romantic relationships. Many people don't become interested in dating until their high school years or later. There's no rush. Do what feels right to you—not your friends or other people you know. If your friends are intense about dating and are pressuring you, explain to them how you feel. If they continue to push you, you may need to look around for friends who share your values and beliefs.

"Everybody has a right to be treated with respect."
**—Julio, 13**

*Chicken Soup for the Soul: Teens Talk Middle School: 101 Stories of Life, Love, and Learning for Younger Teens* by Jack Canfield. This book has stories from real tweens and teens about all kinds of middle school topics, including relationships.

*Real Friends vs. the Other Kind* by Annie Fox. Learn insider information on making friends, gossip, exclusion, cyberbullying, crushes, peer pressure, and other topics.

## Your First Kiss

When you were younger, the idea of a romantic kiss probably seemed sort of gross. But lately, it may not seem that way at all. In fact, now that you've entered the middle school years, you may be very curious about kissing—and hoping your first kiss will happen soon.

During the next few years, you may find yourself in more kissing situations. For example, you may be invited to parties where the entertainment includes kissing games like Spin the Bottle. Participating in these kinds of activities isn't required. If you don't feel ready to kiss someone in a game like this, you can say so. If the people you're with are true friends and they respect your point of view, they'll understand.

On the other hand, maybe you're eagerly looking forward to the chance to kiss someone you like. You probably see a lot of kissing on TV and in movies. In fact, by now you've probably seen hundreds of on-screen "smooches" that take place in romantic settings with swelling music. Is real-life kissing like that? Sometimes. But the perfect kissing you see on TV and in movies is completely scripted and planned out. The actors—who've been carefully made up, dressed, lighted, and filmed by professionals—have rehearsed every move.

Many people your age wonder what kissing feels like or how to kiss the "right" way. Some practice their kissing techniques on pillows or on their arms or hands. But the best preparation of all is knowing you're ready to kiss or be kissed.

Kissing can happen almost anywhere and at any time. Maybe you're just talking to your boyfriend or girlfriend, or you're getting ready to say good-bye after having spent a fun day together—suddenly there might be a pause, and the moment seems right. Move toward the other person gently, which is a way to ask without words whether it's okay. If the other person seems willing, go ahead and kiss. (Otherwise, *stop*.) When you're kissing, try not to judge the experience too much. Lots of first kisses involve colliding foreheads, noses, or braces.

A note about kissing and telling: it's natural to want to tell your friends about your kissing experiences, but remember, the person you kissed may not want the details spread all over school. Some things are best kept to yourself.

## A Closing Thought . . .

During the next few years, you'll probably face all sorts of new "firsts"—your first school dance, crush, or kiss, for example. These firsts can be exciting. Others may be very hard-to-handle—like your first experience with intense peer pressure or a clique, or your first big fight with a friend. You won't always know how things will turn out, but you can do your best to be prepared.

Talk to some adults or older siblings about what to expect and how to handle new situations you might face. Even more important, ask yourself what's right for you when it comes to friendship, peer pressure, dating, and other aspects of the middle school social scene. Do you know what's important to you? Do you know how to take care of yourself? To stick up for yourself or stand up for what you believe? Think about these and you'll find it a lot easier to stay true to you!

# Make the Most
# of Middle School

Why make the most of middle school? One good reason is the amount of time you spend there. How many hours do you spend getting ready in the morning, going to class, finishing homework, and participating in sports, clubs, or other activities? School takes up a large chunk of your life! School should be more than just a place to see your friends (although that's not a bad start)—and definitely more than something you have to "get through." This is where **Survival Tip #6** comes in. You'll find ideas for making homework more bearable, doing well on tests, working on projects, taking part in activities, and discovering how to enjoy learning.

# Surviving Middle School

Middle school is different from elementary school. You may have had different teachers for special classes like art or gym in elementary school, but now you probably have a different teacher for every subject. The upside is that each teacher is a specialist in a particular area: Your science teacher will have lots of training in science, just as your social studies teacher will have special knowledge of history and government. Is there a downside? Perhaps that it's a little harder to get to know your teachers—and help them get to know you—when you see them for less than an hour each day.

Another difference is that many middle schools have homerooms. This will be your home base at school and the first place you go each morning. Homerooms, or advisory time, serve as important sources of information (attendance, announcements, sign-ups) for you. Your homeroom teacher will most likely teach you in at least one other class.

Along with a homeroom, you may also be assigned to a locker. This is your place to store all the notebooks, folders, and textbooks you're not using at the moment. If your locker doesn't already come with a combination lock, you can buy one. Memorize the combination and practice using

"I thought middle school would be harder, but it's actually easier than fifth grade. I like having different teachers, study hall, and more choices."
—**Jana, 11**

"The first month was a little hard. Getting to my locker, remembering the combination and what books I needed, and getting to know different teachers. . . . But now I've adjusted and I like it."
—**Tamara, 12**

"Don't be afraid that no one will help you in middle school. If you ask enough people, someone is sure to have the answer or assistance you need."
—**Rob, 14**

the lock before putting everything you own in your locker. If you have two lockers, one for books and one for gym clothes, you may want to buy a pair of locks with the same combination (they're sold as a set).

Another change from your elementary days is the amount of class-work, homework, projects, and tests you'll have. Now that you're older, you can handle more assignments. But you'll have to plan your time much more carefully, especially if you tend to feel stressed out when you have a lot to do.

One of the biggest differences in middle school is that you're expected to find your own way. You're not led around by an adult who

 **Getting Settled In at School**

Feeling nervous on the first day of middle school is normal. Being prepared helps, so try the following tips:

- Talk to other students who've already gone through at least one year at your middle school to find out the most important things you'll need to know.

- Find out where the bathrooms are before you need to get to one in a hurry. Also practice opening your locker.

- Be sure you know your parents' work or cell phone numbers along with the names and numbers of other people you can call in an emergency.

- Remember to bring a lunch, or bring money or a voucher, to buy one at the cafeteria. (Having your mom or dad show up with your forgotten lunch isn't the best way to make a good first impression.)

- Bring the supplies you need, including pens, notebooks, laptop, binders, planners, and any other items your school requires.

- Know your schools' rules on cell phones. Stash yours in your locker if you have one with you but aren't supposed to.

makes sure you're handling your assignments properly or getting to your next class on time. This doesn't mean you're entirely on your own. Teachers, administrators, guidance counselors, and other adults are all there to help you. The key here is you have to ask for it.

Many schools schedule an orientation in the spring or summer—long before the first day of middle school. Sometimes the first day is also an orientation. That's the time to find out critical pieces of information, like the location of the nurse's office, bathrooms, and your locker. Take notes during orientation and keep any handouts you've been given, since you may forget important details over the summer.

"In elementary school, boys and girls are walked to the library or wherever they're going. In middle school, you're told, 'Now everybody, just get to the library.' There's no teacher or hall monitor following you."

**—Juanita, 13**

## Getting Along with Teachers

Teachers are people, and people have a wide range of personalities, attitudes, and likes and dislikes. You'll get along better with some than others, just as you do with your classmates. Teachers want you to succeed—they don't believe it's their job to torture you (even if it may sometimes seem that way). Think of it this way: the more successful you are in school, the more successful your teachers feel. Try to think of you and your teachers as partners in learning.

Just as you want teachers to be fair with you, they also have expectations of you. These are behaviors they feel are important for class. Here are some ways to get off on the right foot with teachers:

**Be on time.** Tardiness is a major pet peeve for many teachers. To make a good impression, get to class on time. Also let teachers know in advance if you'll be late or absent.

**Come to class prepared.** Another thing that can really annoy teachers is when students don't come to class with the books, homework, or supplies they need. Before going to class, double-check that you have everything you need.

**Be respectful.** When you're respectful toward teachers, they are much more likely to show *you* respect and treat you well.

**Pay attention.** It might sound simple, but a lot of students upset teachers by not listening in class. Most teachers care about the subjects they are teaching, so when people don't seem interested they may take offense. Moving to the front of the room (instead of sitting at the back) is one thing that can improve attention.

**Ask questions.** Use questions to show interest in what you're learning. Teachers appreciate when students show genuine curiosity about school topics. It makes them feel like they're doing a good job. You can also ask questions to get to know teachers better.

**Remember that every teacher is different.** Figure out what a teacher thinks is important. If a certain teacher expects class participation, make an extra effort to get involved in class discussions. If another teacher believes neatness is crucial, work hard to hand in papers that don't look messy. If getting your work finished on time is important to one of your teachers, do your best to meet deadlines.

It's important to do your part in building good relationships with teachers. And it really is worth the effort. A teacher can be your mentor, helping you discover what you love to do and encouraging you to pursue your talents. A teacher can also be like a friend—someone to go to when you have a problem at school or in your personal life. And a great teacher can even inspire you to be great yourself!

Sometimes in the process of getting to know a teacher—especially one who's really terrific, young, or attractive—you may develop a crush. This happens often, but it is usually temporary. Daydreaming about your teacher or a coach is normal (even typical) at your age, but acting on this type of romantic fantasy is never okay. If you're confused about your feelings for your teacher or uncomfortable with something he or she has said or done to you, talk to an adult you trust.

What about teachers you don't like? Or just can't seem to get along with no matter how hard you try? One good thing about middle school is that you don't have to spend all day with those teachers you have trouble with. That might not make you feel better if a teacher who yells a lot or is highly critical ruins your entire day. If the situation is unbearable, ask a parent or school official to get involved.

> "Your teachers expect much more from you now than they did in elementary school. But most of them are willing to help if you're willing to approach them."
> —**Gabriella**, 13

> "My favorite teacher was like a kid in many ways. She would do impersonations of things and people. She was fun, but at the same time, she made you work hard."
> —**Chen**, 11

## Brain Power

Your teachers expect more from you in middle school because just as your body is growing and changing, so is your brain. You can probably remember all kinds of facts, statistics, dates, and formulas—thousands of pieces of information in your brain ready for action when needed. Digging through this growing warehouse of information allows you to figure out the answers on tests or to do your homework problems. Not only do you have more information available to help you answer questions, but you're also developing more complex ways of thinking and solving problems.

**FAST FACT**

What do a healthy diet, regular physical activity, and a good night's sleep have to do with succeeding at school? Plenty. Research shows that students who are active, eat well, and sleep at least eight hours a night perform better at school. When you take care of your body, your brain also gets a power boost, which makes it easier for you to stay alert, process information, and show your creativity.

Maybe you've also found that, once in a while, you just can't retrieve a specific piece of information at the precise moment you need it. How many times has it happened to you: You're taking a test, and you can almost see the fact on the page, but it just doesn't come into clear enough focus? After the test, you rush to the text-book and, of course, there it is, clear as day—the formula you needed. This can be pretty frustrating, but the good news is you'll probably remember that fact for a long time.

Learning something well is a way to retain information, instead of just memorizing facts for a test. Learning involves constant reviewing. You may have to read something again and again before it sinks in. You may also have to write it down to remember it. And after that, you may still need to review the information several times before you finally get it. (Check out the "Study SMART" tips on page 125.)

## Different Ways of Learning

Does music help you study, or does it distract you? Have you found that you learn better when you have an opportunity to do something, rather than just listen to a lecture? Maybe a friend takes in information best by reading, but you like presentations. You, like everybody else, have your own best way to learn.

In addition to having a preferred way to learn, you know you're more talented in some areas than in others. In a middle school class-room of twenty-five students, a few may have special abilities in math or music, while others may show superior athletic skills. Some may be gifted in the way they understand and deal with people, while some may have a knack for writing and communicating. Some students are strong in many areas, while others are exceptionally talented in one particular skill.

Take a moment to think about your own strengths. What do you get excited to learn about? What do you love to do? Is there a certain class you shine in? Are most classes easy or hard for you? Is school enough of a challenge? Are you feeling bored in some classes?

If you feel that you want more of a challenge, here are some suggestions:

- Think of ways to make your assignments more exciting. Instead of writing a paper about how skyscrapers are built, for example, you could create a model of one.

- Get involved in an after-school activity—perhaps a theater group, the school newspaper, or the chess club. This can help you feel more creative and interested in what your school has to offer.

- Ask your guidance counselor about opportunities for advanced study open to middle school students. Local high schools, colleges, or universities, for example, may offer summer programs. You might also be able to get involved in a long-distance program in math, writing, a foreign language, or another subject.

- Find out if your school has a program for gifted and talented students. Talk to your teacher about whether you may be qualified.

## When Learning Is Difficult

For some students, school is a real struggle. If you're having a tough time, you know how discouraging it is to put a lot of effort into your work and still do poorly. You may need to learn different strategies for taking notes or studying. A guidance counselor or a teacher may be able to help. If your school has a tutoring program, try that out. Ask your mom or dad for help in a subject that's giving you trouble. Some students do better using a laptop than writing their notes. Others may need to sit up front closer to the teacher. You may need to try a few of these options before you notice an improvement in your grades.

*The Survival Guide for Kids with ADD or ADHD* by John F. Taylor. Find information here on ADD and ADHD as well as strategies for enjoying school, making friends, and getting along at home.

*The Survival Guide for Kids with LD (Learning Differences)* by Gary Fisher and Rhoda Cummings. This book has information on learning differences and tips for succeeding in school and the years beyond.

Some students have learning difficulties. This doesn't mean they're stupid or can't learn. Instead, these students process information, perceive words, or recognize numbers differently than other students. There are many types of learning difficulties and many ways to help overcome them to make learning easier. If you need extra help at school, let a teacher, parent, or school counselor know. Schools are required by law to help students with learning difficulties.

# Studying Smart and Succeeding at Homework

Changing classes can be fun, but more classes can also mean more homework and tests. In elementary school, the teacher went over the homework list and made sure you'd packed the books you needed before the final bell rang. Now, you are more independent, which brings more responsibility. You'll need to track your assignments, know the resources you need, and juggle deadlines.

Some students seem to just breeze through their homework and barely need to open a book before a test, but most have to study hard to do well. Here are some ways to use your study time well:

**Get organized.** How can you study if the place where you do your homework is a mess? Spending time looking for a pencil or a dictionary can be a waste. If you have your own room, clean up your desk and keep it neat and organized. If you share a room, keep a box or crate with your homework supplies handy and tote them to a quiet spot.

**Make sure you have the tools you need.** Did you bring your textbooks and assignments home? (Teachers hate it when students use the old excuse that they couldn't do their homework because they forgot to bring home their books!) Do you need a calculator for your math problems? Will you have to do research online? Do you have access to a computer or an encyclopedia? If you don't have all the tools you need, can you get a ride to the library or borrow materials from a friend?

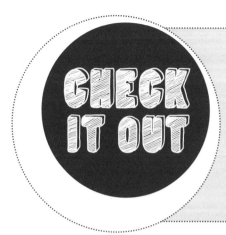

**B.J. Pinchbeck's Homework Helper**
**www.bjpinchbeck.com**
Visit this site for links to educational content and games in virtually every school subject.

**Homework NYC**
**www.homeworkNYC.org**
Operated by the public libraries of New York City, this site features study notes, homework help, and links to other online sources.

**Pick a quiet spot with few distractions.** Make a rule that when you study, you won't turn on the TV or take any phone calls. If you don't want to miss your favorite television show, you can watch it later. Music is a "maybe"—some people can study with music on, while others find it distracting. Being on the computer can also be tough, especially if you know your friends are online. Figure out what works best for you.

**Make sure you have a good reading light and a comfortable chair.** It's not helpful to struggle to see in dim light or strain your shoulders or back while sitting in a chair that's too hard, too soft, or the wrong size for your desk or table.

**Keep a study calendar.** Use a calendar or daily planner—written or electronic (most cell phones have them)—to record your assignment due dates and to track the times and days you plan to study. Each time you make a study date with yourself, do your best to stick to it.

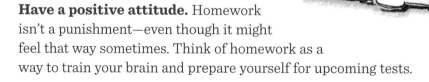

**Have a positive attitude.** Homework isn't a punishment—even though it might feel that way sometimes. Think of homework as a way to train your brain and prepare yourself for upcoming tests.

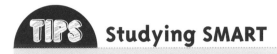

## Studying SMART

Want to study SMART? Here's how:

- **S**kim the chapter headings, the notes at the back of the chapters, and any charts and graphs.
- **M**ake a note of the main points and important details of each chapter as you read.
- **A**sk yourself questions as you go along to see if you understand the material.
- **R**eview your notes and underline the important information.
- **T**ake a break every thirty or forty minutes. Then see what you can remember before you start studying SMART again.

# Taking Tests

It's 10 p.m., and you have a science test tomorrow. Do you break out in a sweat just thinking about it? Or did you start worrying as soon as your teacher announced it? Is your heart pounding now just reading about tests?

Tests are a regular part of middle school life. You probably have more tests now than you did in elementary school—sometimes you may have more than one in a week. That's why test anxiety can become a regular part of the middle school experience for many students.

Getting somewhat anxious about tests is normal. It may help to know that a little fear can actually be a good thing. The stress you feel can motivate you to study and do your best. If you're too relaxed about an upcoming test, you might not bother studying at all, and this could lower your score.

Some middle school students get so anxious that they can barely concentrate before or during a test. This type of fear isn't productive—in fact, it can make success nearly impossible. If you're extremely anxious about test-taking, here are some things you can do to prevent the fear from making you forget even your own name:

**Study.** This is an obvious tip, but it's also the most helpful one. The more you know about a subject, the more comfortable you'll feel going into the test. Over-prepare if you think it might help. Use the SMART tips on page 125.

**Talk to your parents.** They've been in lots of test situations themselves and may have some helpful hints you can try. (If they don't, you've at least given them an opportunity to go down memory lane, something most parents love to do.) Ask them to quiz you or help you better understand the material.

**Talk to your teacher.** Let your teacher know about your fears and ask if he or she can offer tips for calming down. You can also ask for suggestions about what to study.

**Learn some easy relaxation exercises you can do before and even during a test.** Try this one: Close your eyes, imagine a pleasant scene—riding an ocean wave or laughing with friends, for example—and take a couple of deep breaths. Then open your eyes and go back to your test. (See pages 49–54 for more information about reducing stress.)

**Tell yourself you can do well.** (Do this quietly during the test.) If you say things like, "I know the formula for energy" instead of, "I know I'm going to fail this test," you'll feel more confident. In fact, you might be amazed at the difference positive thinking can make!

**Create and take practice tests at home.** This helps you get into your teacher's head. What is she likely to ask? Try answering those questions. What is she not likely to ask? Try answering those questions as well (especially if you're not a talented mind-reader). Some teachers may even provide a practice test, if you ask for one.

**Form a study group with some friends.** Each member can spend some time acting as the teacher. One of the best ways to learn a subject is to explain it to others. Discuss the material and quiz each other. Take breaks every so often to keep yourselves interested and alert.

**Tell yourself it's just one test.** (There will be lots more!) If you mess up or don't do as well as you'd like, remind yourself that it's just one test—not the end of the world.

Successful athletes say that the ability to forget about a misstep is one of the keys to doing well. A basketball player who misses an easy shot can't keep focusing on his error if he wants to play well during the rest of the game. When a figure skater falls in the middle of a routine, she doesn't just lie there on the ice (unless, of course, she's broken her leg). She gets up, continues to skate, and thinks about what's next instead of what went wrong. In both cases, the athletes put the mistake behind them and focus on the rest of their performance. You can do the same in test situations.

 ## Getting Ready for Standardized Tests

Some middle school kids think standardized tests are difficult because they have multiple-choice questions on everything they're supposed to know about one subject. It's hard to figure out what specific questions will be asked. These tests are used to measure the progress you're making in school. You might feel some stress before taking these tests, but take a deep breath, stay calm, and use the tips in this section to do your best.

# Successful School Projects

A project is just the "extra large, extra cheese, extra pepperoni pizza" of homework. Slice it up, and you can finish it in no time—without upsetting your stomach! Here's how:

1. Are you doing this project with a team? If you're working with a group, try to decide what your piece of the project will be as soon as possible.

2. Find a way to make the project interesting for you. For example, if the environment is important to you, your science project could focus on that. Think you'd like to be a doctor someday? Try a project about the human body. Adore animals? Into sports? A music lover? A techno-whiz? Let your project mirror your hobbies and interests, so it's more fun for you to do.

3. Once you know your part of the project (or if you're working alone), break the entire assignment into smaller tasks and set a deadline for completing each one. For example, you may need to do some research, so your first goal could be to schedule research time on Wednesday. By Saturday, organize the information you've collected and see what other research you may need to do.

4. If you're working with a group, make a schedule. Meet regularly at a place with few or no distractions—the mall would not be a good place to work, of course.

5. Make the project look good. If it's a research paper, make sure it's neat and think about using a folder, a binder, or a cover page. Consider fun, unusual, or artistic ways to present your information. Many projects are done as presentations using a computer.

6. Set a date to finish the project at least one week before it's due. An early deadline allows you time to look over your work and make any necessary changes.

7. Giving a presentation? Practice in front of an audience (your family or some close friends who promise not to make you laugh).

8. Using a computer or making a video? Be sure your equipment is working and available. You don't want to find out at the last minute the tools you need for the project aren't working.

9. Doing an experiment? Make sure it works and that all your supplies are ready to go.

10. Finished! Reward yourself for a job well done, and then look forward to the next time you can show off your project skills.

Working on a project with a partner or within a group is typical at most middle schools. Pairing up this way can be a good tool, because as you and your partner share information, you gain knowledge. Teaching others reinforces your own understanding of a subject.

Most teachers try to be fair about how students are grouped, making sure that everyone has a partner, and that different people get a chance to work with each other. But not every partnership turns out to be a successful one. You may feel that you've been assigned to a partner or group that will be difficult to work with. Before judging, give the other person or people a chance. You may change your mind about the situation once you get to know each other better.

Here are some more tips on pairing up for school projects:

- If the teacher assigns partners and you've been overlooked, speak up. Your teacher has a lot of students to manage and may not notice if you've been left out by mistake. A teacher who isn't aware you don't have a partner can't help you.

- If you're allowed to choose partners, look for someone who can complement your strengths. Suppose you know a student who's a good writer and you have artistic skills—just imagine the possibilities if the two of you were partners.

- Once you have a partner, spend time learning more about each other's interests and talents. What can you each add to this joint project? Maybe you're great at building things or you know how to organize a report well—don't be shy about mentioning what you're good at.

- Do your share as a partner, but don't overdo (or underdo) it. Pull your weight, even volunteering for some of the less-appealing parts of the project. But don't take over, even if you believe your talents will help your team earn an A. Part of the reason for working with others is learning to cooperate and complete something together.

- Whether you're working on a project with a group or alone, start by doing some brainstorming. You can use the exercise on the next page to come up with ideas for topics, research, and more.

## Project Ideas

On the computer or a piece of paper, keep track of all your ideas for doing projects as well as what you'll have to do to complete them. You might track the following information:

- Topic ideas
- Title ideas
- Supplies and books needed
- Research to be done
- People to interview
- Steps to take along with dates for completion
- Presentation ideas
- Project due date

# Preparing Reports

You may have done a few reports in elementary school, but in middle school, reports are a *bigger* deal. They're longer, for starters. And you may be expected to use more resources for your research. In addition, middle school teachers expect you to use even more creativity when putting together reports. Are you up to the task? Sure you are!

Reports, like school projects, are hard work and they demand a lot of time. As with school projects, breaking down the assignment into steps can help. Start with a brainstorming session and figure out what topics you'd like to explore. Make a long list, writing down any ideas that pop into your head, no matter how off-the-wall they may seem. Read over the ideas and choose the ones that appeal to you most. Now ask yourself these questions: Can I find enough information on this topic? Will too many others in the class be tackling this topic, too? Try to pick an idea that's not only original but will also be possible to research. If your teacher has already assigned the topic, brainstorm new and different ways to present it.

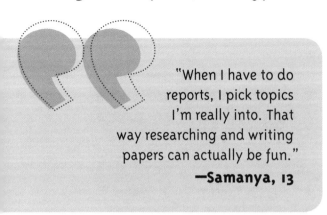

"When I have to do reports, I pick topics I'm really into. That way researching and writing papers can actually be fun."
**—Samanya, 13**

You can do research using books and magazines, or by searching the Internet. You can find educational publishers, encyclopedias, museums, and university libraries online.

Whether you're doing your research electronically or with print publications, follow these basics:

**Don't try to read every word of a website, article, or chapter you've found.** Instead, skim to see if you've located the exact information you need, and then make notes. Keep printouts or photocopies of the materials, if possible, so you can refer to them later if needed. Or bookmark the sources or copy and paste the links onto one page.

**Don't plagiarize.** Plagiarizing is copying word-for-word the information you've found and putting it into your report. By law, you can only copy the words if you're quoting the material and using footnotes. Bookmark the Internet sites that seem useful. This will also help with your footnotes. Learn from other people's ideas, but then express those ideas in your own words.

**Don't copy and paste from a website or report you find online.** Most schools have programs that check student work to see if it is plagiarized. Besides the risk of getting caught, cheating is just lazy and wrong.

**Analyze your research to decide if it's useful or helpful.** Some websites are very accurate but others aren't. Ask questions like: Is this a reliable source? Is the information current? Is it accurate? Is it complete?

After you've finished researching, you're ready to make an outline to follow. What information do you want to cover? Which ideas should be presented first? What comes next? After that? What conclusions can you draw? An outline can guide you through the writing process.

Next, you can begin to write. At this point, you don't need to worry about spelling, grammar, or making "perfect" sentences. Just get your ideas down in a first draft. When you're done with that draft, read it carefully so you can make revisions. And remember that no one—not even famous authors—writes a perfect first draft.

Are you happy with what you've written? Did you express yourself clearly? Did you follow your outline? Is there any information you left out that should be added? Anything you want to delete? Make any final changes, and then begin to check your grammar and spelling.

Many computer programs have spellchecks that will help you spot errors. Even so, don't depend on your computer to catch every misspelled word. Review your report carefully because your computer will read a word like *he* as spelled correctly, when you really meant to type *the*. You can also have your computer check your grammar, but as with the spellcheck, it's not always the best "proofer." Be sure to review your work carefully yourself, and even ask a family member to look it over for mistakes, too.

Your family and friends can also help you determine if your report is complete and interesting. Ask somebody you trust to read the report and offer comments. Try not to get discouraged by any criticism you might receive. Instead, look at it as feedback that can help you make your work even better.

**Carnegie Library Homework Help**
**www.carnegielibrary.org/kids/bigkids/homework**
Research tips, live homework help, links, and educational games make this a great school resource.

**Encyclopedia Britannica**
**www.britannica.com**
This online encyclopedia, featuring updated articles, videos, and a blog, is a great reference for projects and reports.

Allow time to do a final rewrite. You may think of ways to make your writing clearer, or you may want to add a fact you forgot. When you're happy with the rewrite, decide how you're going to "format" your report (how you want it to look). Most reports are printed in a twelve-point font or type. Check that your margins are even and include page numbers if you need them. You can add a "header" or "footer" that will print your name, the title of your report, and the page number on every sheet. The better you get at formatting, the more interesting you can make your reports look!

Graphics and tables also add interest to school reports. Depending on the computer and software you're using, you can turn your report into a presentation, video, or movie. You can add photos, too. Remember, just as with words, images may be copyrighted, too. Include information on where the image came from or use copyright-free images. Programs for drawing, painting, or designing on screen allow you to make adjustments to your photos and text. Add some music, and you can create a multimedia extravaganza that will surely dazzle your teacher and classmates!

A word of warning: Always be sure to save your work and have a backup before you print a copy. You can even set the computer to automatically save your work every five minutes or so. This will prevent you from experiencing a major school-report disaster—like losing everything you've written!

**Getting Help from Your Family**

Parents and older siblings at home can do a lot to help support you as a student. They might:

- help create a well-lighted, quiet, private work space for you at home
- suggest books and websites you can look at for homework help or information for a report or project
- brainstorm ideas with you when you're trying to figure out a topic or a strategy for a report or project
- look at an outline you've prepared before you start the actual writing of a report or paper
- review your paper or project after you've finished a draft and suggest minor changes (don't have them rewrite—that will improve only their writing skills)
- ask you questions to help you review for a quiz or test
- review a test you've already taken to help you understand why certain answers were marked wrong
- celebrate a great report card with you (not with gifts or money, but with congratulations on a job well done)
- encourage you to work harder when you receive a grade that's below your potential
- listen to you when you gripe about a teacher, test, or classmate, and then offer advice for handling the situation
- suggest ways you might talk to a teacher in a class you're having trouble with, or one in which a classmate is bothering you
- help you brainstorm ways to make school more challenging
- act as an advocate for you when you're in a difficult situation at school (meaning they might talk to your teacher, a guidance counselor, or even the principal)
- read this list, so they'll know what you now know about how they can best help you in school!

# Extracurricular Activities in Middle School

Middle school isn't just about tests, reports, and homework. Most schools provide students with many opportunities for extracurricular activities—before or after school and on weekends.

Athletics are a major part of the school experience for many students. For some, joining a team is the most natural thing in the world. Maybe they've been playing soccer or softball since their elementary school days. Other kids don't like sports or consider themselves to be athletic. The good news is that middle school has opportunities for people with all kinds of interests, including drama, debate, band, and many other activities.

# Playing Sports

If you happen to have talent for a sport or a strong desire to play, you can look into joining a community travel team. These teams choose players through a competitive tryout system. Travel teams play against other teams in an area—sometimes a very large area. Travel teams often take trips to other cities, or even other states, for games or tournaments. If the idea of competition and hard work excites you, you might want to consider trying out for a travel team. You can talk to your gym teacher or the local parks and recreation department to find out where and when to try out.

If you're interested in a sport but don't want to make a big commitment (like getting up at dawn on a cold Saturday to prepare for a game), a travel team probably wouldn't be right for you. Instead, you might look into other sporting opportunities. Many communities and schools organize intramural teams, which are less competitive than travel teams (at least in the way people qualify). Most intramural teams are set up to allow people of all abilities to play. So if you've been wanting to try basketball but haven't had a lot of playing time, you could join an intramural team. See if your gym teacher has information for you, or ask some others at school or in your neighborhood. Some middle school students join both intramural and travel teams. Because teams are often determined randomly, be prepared to play against your close friends.

School teams are often less competitive than travel squads, but more intense than intramural athletics. You may have to try out, but these teams often don't require the kind of time commitment that travel teams do. To find out what kind of team experience might be best for you (and your family), take the following quiz.

## TRY IT · Team Quiz

Directions: On the computer or a sheet of paper, write whether you: strongly disagree, disagree, agree, or strongly agree with each statement.

1. I don't mind getting up very early on a weekend if I can play on a good team.
2. Receiving tough criticism really bothers me.
3. My family is willing and able to take me to games and practices, even at night and on weekends.
4. Sports are important to me but not one of my top three interests.
5. My friends say I'm a great athlete.
6. I'm not a very competitive person.
7. I'm good at managing my time.
8. I'm in pretty good physical shape, and I'm prepared to work hard to stay that way.
9. I wouldn't want to have to devote myself to one sport more than another.
10. Focusing on academics is way more important to me than being a top athlete.

**What do your answers mean?**

If you agreed with statements 1, 3, 5, 7, and 8, you're a good candidate for a travel team. If you strongly agreed with at least three of them, travel teams are probably ideal for you.

If you agreed with statements 2, 4, 6, 9, and 10, you might enjoy an intramural team. And if you strongly agreed with those items, intramural team, here you come!

## Joining Clubs and Community Activities

Besides sports, you can do many other activities through school clubs and community programs. Here's your chance to try something new. Maybe being in the school play wasn't your thing in fourth grade, but choosing the drama class—as an actor or a stage crew member—sounds interesting today. During after-school time, you could try music classes, chess, debate, or community service.

If you're not sure of the activities you want to do, try a few to see which are a good fit. In addition to school opportunities, you can also seek fun through religious organizations, health clubs, or youth groups. You might start by checking out the Boys and Girls Clubs (www.bgca.org), Girl Scouts (www.girlscouts.org), or Boy Scouts (www.scouting.org). Middle school is a great time to try out clubs and activities—you're still not as busy as you will be in high school and you don't need to be an expert to take part.

# Preparing for the Years and Careers Ahead

You already know that the study habits you develop now will prepare you for your life as a high school or college student. And if you're not too pleased with those habits (or the grades you've been getting), you might want to go back to some of the information earlier in this chapter for a brief refresher course.

It's not too early to start thinking about high school and college. The courses you take now are the foundation for the subjects you'll study in high school. And some students will even have an opportunity to take high-school-level courses

> "I never thought I was great at writing, but now I really like it. I am making up stories all the time and I joined the school paper. I think I'd like to be a writer."
> **—Tonya, 13**

while they're still in middle school. Make an appointment with your school guidance counselor or advisor to find out about special opportunities. For example, if you receive very high scores on standardized tests, you'll be able to take a more advanced standardized exam while you're in seventh or eighth grade and be eligible for special programs during the summer and by mail or computer during the school year. If you want to go to college, be sure to start taking the kinds of classes that will best prepare you for the high school courses that are important for college.

In addition to thinking about the school years ahead, you may start wondering about career possibilities. You may already have a good idea about what kind of work you'd like to do—or not. Either way, you have lots of time before you actually have to decide. And once you're working, it's likely that you'll make a couple of job shifts as your interests, needs, or circumstances change.

Is there a job you're dreaming about, but you wonder if it's too far out of your reach? Maybe you love to sing or dance, but those careers seem so competitive that you're wondering if you should become an accountant instead. Or maybe you want to be a poet, but people are already telling you that you'll need to get a "real job" first. Perhaps you want to own your own company, come up with an amazing invention, or help solve the world's hunger problem. Don't ever give

> "I want to be a teacher. I'd make my classes fun and students would learn a lot, too. The best teachers I had did that and in middle school I see the difference a good teacher makes."
> —**Matthew**, 11

> "I'm using a computer a lot more now—for school and for fun. My middle school has a technology program that continues in high school, and I am going to talk to my home base teacher about signing up."
> —**Carla**, 12

up on a dream—even one that doesn't seem to have a high probability of success. If you want something badly enough, it's worth it to try to make it happen!

Maybe you have no idea what you want to do with your future. Or perhaps you have so many interests that it's hard to imagine one particular path. What can you do now to explore various career options? Here are some ideas:

- Take advantage of a school holiday to go to work for a day with a parent or another adult family member.

- Read biographies or autobiographies of successful people in a variety of careers.

- Join school clubs or get involved in extracurricular activities (such as making costumes or building sets for the school play) to get some experience in areas you haven't yet investigated.

- Practice skills that will be important in any job—time management, assertiveness, conflict resolution, problem solving, and decision making. It's never too early to get a handle on these skills.

- Many schools have collections of career videos for students. Check with a librarian, teacher, or guidance counselor to see if yours does.

- Remind yourself of how much time you'll spend at work during your lifetime—and how important it is to pursue a career that will be fun and challenging. People who work because they love what they do are always the most satisfied in their careers.

## A Closing Thought . . .

As a middle school student, you're developing habits, skills, and ideas that will set the stage for your success in high school, college, and beyond. You can see school as a place you hate to go (and an experience you have to get through), or you can view it as a place that can help you develop your mind, your body, your talents, and your interests. Part of getting older is recognizing that you can turn these opportunities into accomplishments.

# Take Charge
## of Your Life

Change. That's what the middle school years are all about. Changes
affect your body, appearance, feelings, family relationships, friendships, and school day. So much change can make it hard to feel in
control. It might feel like everything is new and that it's becoming
harder to decide what you want or what's best for you. What can you
do to stay on track and be true to who you are? **Survival Tip #7** is all
about taking charge of your life.

# Make Decisions Right for You

The older you get, the more decisions you need to make and the more difficult decisions become. When you were younger, your family made many decisions for you—even picking out the clothes you wore and the activities you participated in. But as you get older, you take on more of the decision making. You become more independent. And with your growing independence come some difficult choices.

As you know, all decisions are not the same. Some are pretty easy, like what you're going to eat for breakfast. Others are harder. Maybe two friends have separately invited you to do something Friday night. It might be up to you to decide what to do without making one of them upset. And some decisions can be very hard to make. Perhaps your dad and stepmom want you to visit during school break, but you don't want to leave town.

Every decision involves a choice. You have to choose what to do or what to say (or sometimes you may choose to do or say nothing). Making the best choice can be difficult. But you can follow a set of decision-making steps to help the process go more smoothly.

"Sometimes I think it was easier being a little kid and being told what to do. Deciding things on my own isn't always easy."
—**Cody, 11**

"I have a really hard time deciding what to do. Even after I ask my sister, mom, and best friend, I still can't decide what's best. I think that's just part of being twelve, maybe."
—**Satina, 12**

"I like having more control over my life. It feels good to know that adults have trust in me. And that I can earn more responsibility by showing I'm ready for it."
—**Ezra, 14**

**1. Decide what the real issues are.** Suppose you don't want to visit your dad and stepmom during your school break. Ask yourself the reason why—and be honest about it. Do you not want to go because you and your friends have made exciting plans? Or is it because you still feel upset about your parents' divorce and your father's remarriage?

Knowing what the true problem is can help you make the best decision. If your reason for not going is because you're angry with your dad, then not going may be a bad decision. You'll hurt him, and ultimately yourself, because the two of you won't have a chance to work on your relationship. If your reason for not going is because you have a heavy schedule of sports and other activities with friends, then not going may be a good decision. You need to fulfill your responsibilities to your teammates, and you may be able to visit your dad during the next school break instead.

How do you figure out what the real issue is? You can:

- talk about your dilemma with family members and friends
- write about your problem in your journal
- set aside some quiet time to reflect on your choices
- discuss your feelings with a sympathetic and trusted adult—a school counselor, youth group leader, or teacher, for example

**2. Review your options.** Make a list of the choices you have before you. If two friends want to get together with you on the same night, you could:

- go out with one friend and tell the other no
- stay home
- suggest the three of you do something as a group

If your decision is a difficult one, consider the pros and cons of each option. Write them down, think about them carefully, or discuss them with a neutral person. Here are some examples.

Going out with one friend: the pro is that you'd make one friend happy, but the con is that your other friend may have hurt feelings.

Staying home: the pro is you don't have to say no to anyone, but the cons are that you might not have much fun alone and your friends may be disappointed.

Doing something as a group: the pro is you all get to have a good time—maybe there's no con!

**3. Make your decision.** Set a reasonable deadline for yourself— anywhere from an hour to a week, depending on the difficulty of the decision. Then pick one of the actions from your list and follow it.

Sometimes, even when you make the best decision you can, you may not get the results you wanted. This can be a learning opportunity.

Suppose you have to decide between continuing piano lessons or taking voice lessons instead. You talk to your family and your music teacher to get their opinions. You write in your journal about what to do. You list the pros and cons, set a deadline, and make a decision to stick with piano. But after a few weeks, you start to wonder if you've made the wrong choice.

Now what? Do you agonize over it or get mad at yourself for picking the wrong thing? No, because you can always make a new decision. Life is full of interesting choices—and each one you make will lead you in a new direction. Sometimes you need to just enjoy the adventure and dis-cover where your decisions will take you!

## FAST FACT

Some scientists, looking at digital exams of the brain, have seen that it continues to grow into a person's twenties. The part of the brain you use to make decisions is one of the last parts to fully develop. So, while that is not a good excuse to use when you don't make the best decision, it is useful to know that sometimes you may need to slow down and really consider the decision you are making. Are you sure you are making the best choice? Take a moment to think it through.

# Take Care of Number One

Taking care of yourself—putting yourself first—means doing what's best for you and your body. That includes:

- eating right and exercising
- avoiding unhealthy habits (like cigarettes, alcohol, and drugs)
- making positive decisions
- being with friends who respect your values and positive choices
- making an effort to manage your time and your schoolwork
- keeping a good relationship with your family
- feeling good about who you are

> "If you have the 'right' friends, they aren't going to pressure you to do the wrong things."
> **—Dontrell, 14**

> "A boy in my class is always talking about smoking, like it's a really big deal. But I think he's just trying to get attention."
> **—Julie, 11**

> "Making good decisions comes down to knowing what's best for you. Sometimes that's not always clear, so you need to figure it out."
> **—Nina, 13**

Making decisions that are the right ones for you can be very difficult if your friends or classmates are making some not-so-good choices themselves. Suppose you want to eat healthy foods, but your friends are "snack-a-holics," consuming junk food at lunch and for snacks. Do you do the same, so you don't stick out? What if your friends are taking illegal drugs, smoking cigarettes, or drinking beer or other types of alcohol? You know these activities are risky, but you don't want to be left out or teased. What do you do?

People often forget to take care of themselves when they feel stressed out or pressured by friends. Even if you know you should eat right or avoid unhealthy activities, you may tell yourself it's easier to just go along with what your friends and other people your age are doing. At other times, you may be talked into stuff because you're tired of disagreeing. And at still other times, you may simply be curious about trying something you haven't tried before—especially if your friends are talking about how "cool" it is.

Take smoking as an example. What if a friend starts smoking and wants you to smoke, too? Maybe you see advertisements that show smokers looking healthy and sophisticated, and you want to look the same way. Perhaps you've seen your favorite movie star smoking, and you think having a cigarette may make you more like the person you admire. Should you give in? Not a chance.

Doing things you don't want to do or giving in to negative peer pressure or media messages means you're putting yourself last. Learn how to stick up for yourself and be assertive. Peer pressure is very intense during the middle school years and being "different" can be hard. But taking care of yourself may mean saying no to the bad decisions your friends and peers are making. The truth is, most people really admire people who are able to stand up for themselves and make decisions that show self-respect. Page 99 ("Handling Peer Pressure") has ideas for doing this.

If you're having a hard time making healthy decisions, talk to family members, teachers, or other trusted adults. Getting the advice of people who care about you can help you make smarter choices.

**Above the Influence**
**www.abovetheinfluence.com**
Visit this site for facts on alcohol and drugs. Videos and other features make it an interesting place to get informed.

**The Cool Spot**
**www.thecoolspot.gov**
Along with information on how illegal substances affect your body, this website features advice on resisting peer pressure.

# Take Healthy Risks

Healthy risks vs. bad risks: How do you tell the difference?

Bad risks are dangerous—they can hurt your body or your mind. For example, attempting a dangerous skateboarding trick without a helmet or knee pads is a bad risk. So is drinking alcohol when you're underage, or taking illegal drugs anytime.

Healthy risks, on the other hand, help you stretch yourself in new ways. For example, maybe you are nervous about performing in front of an audience or participating in a new activity at school, but you go through with it anyway. Positive risks like this are all about trying something you're not 100 percent sure you'll do well—but going for it anyway because you believe in yourself enough to take a chance.

Unlike negative risks (like using drugs or alcohol), healthy risks can have a positive impact on your life. There are all kinds of examples of healthy risks. Some people enjoy physical risks—they're "thrill seekers," and they like the adrenaline rush of extreme sports or other physical feats. Others shy away from these kinds of activities but love challenges such as entering a contest, participating in theater, doing a service project, giving a presentation, or running for a class office. All of these experiences, whether they challenge your body or mind (or both), can be positive risks.

> "I love climbing mountains. So far I've only climbed some smaller ones with my parents. One day, though, I want to take on Mount Everest."
> —Simone, 14

If you're a natural risk taker, it may be easy for you to meet new people or try out the latest roller coaster. Your challenge may be to curb your impulse toward dangerous risk taking—like trying things you're not prepared for physically or mentally.

If you tend to avoid risks of almost any kind, however, you may need to find ways to break out of your comfort zone and explore new opportunities. For example, suppose you love to sing. You sing in the shower, you sing in your room along with your favorite groups—but you would never dare do it in public. What if you forget the words? What if you sing off-key? What if . . . ? The "what ifs" can stop you from taking the good risks that help you grow and add excitement to your life.

At some point during middle school, you may have a chance to run for student government, take the lead on a class project, try out for a sports team, or start your own business—all positive risks. But if you focus on negative what ifs, you might not take the risk at all. Instead of imagining the worst that can happen, consider the best that can happen. Focus on the positive what ifs: What if I succeed? What if I feel really good about myself for taking a chance? What if I build my confidence and self-esteem? That's the way to pump yourself up to try something new.

Not taking the risk to try something you want to do is a lot worse than taking the risk and failing. After all, you can always try again! You can figure out what went wrong and take steps to fix it. And now that you've had at least one "practice run," you'll have a better idea of what (and what not) to do next time.

When you push yourself to take a risk, you learn a lot about yourself and what you're capable of doing. You'll also earn respect from your friends and family for giving something your best shot.

## Make Time for a Hobby

Hobbies are a fun way to take healthy risks by trying new things. You can share a hobby with a friend or family member, or do one on your own. You might choose from all kinds of hobbies—common ones like playing a sport or collecting things, or more unusual ones like bee-keeping. When life seems to be going a mile a minute, a hobby can be a relaxing escape. And when your life is going well, a hobby can add to the fun.

Hobbies are active—they help develop your mind or body. And they give you a way to explore life beyond what you learn in school—good risks. A hobby you have now can stay with you your whole life, like a familiar friend who's always interesting and there for you. Some hobbies may even become careers. If you don't have a hobby or you'd like to find a new one, take the following quiz. Your answers may point to interests you didn't know you had.

# TRY IT   Hobby Quiz

Directions: Pick either A or B for each question. Write out your choices on the computer or a separate sheet of paper.

1. Which would you rather be?
**A** indoors
**B** outdoors

2. Which do you enjoy more?
**A** winning
**B** playing the game

3. Which way do you prefer to spend your free time?
**A** alone
**B** with others

4. Which would you rather do on a vacation?
**A** visit a city and go to museums, shows, and the theater
**B** go hiking and camping in a national forest

5. How do you prefer to contact your friends?
**A** text
**B** notes on your own handmade paper

6. What do you do when you're bored in class?
**A** cover your page with doodles
**B** daydream about being outdoors

7. What's more your style?
**A** pack-rat
**B** neat-freak

continued

8. What do you do while waiting in a long line?
**A** take out the book you brought with you to read
**B** mentally rehearse scoring a goal

9. What do you prefer doing after school?
**A** play ball or do some other physical activity
**B** look at a magazine

10. What do you do if something is broken in your house?
**A** try fixing it yourself
**B** read and explain the directions to a family member who's willing to make the repair

Take a look at your results. Did you choose answers that involve being outdoors or doing something physical? Did you pick ones that show you like to do things with your hands? That you enjoy mental challenges? That you're competitive by nature? Did your answers reveal that you like to be involved with other people? Or that you prefer pursuing activities on your own? Did you learn something new about yourself?

Below is a list of different types of hobbies. Try to find one that matches your interests.

**Creative expression:** watercolor painting, oil painting, murals, sculpture, drawing, photography, creative writing, bookmaking, jewelry-making, poetry, drama, music, singing, needlepoint, woodworking, journaling

**Physical activities:** soccer, hockey, baseball, basketball, football, volleyball, tennis, biking, running, dance, cheerleading, gymnastics, horseback riding, karate, ice skating, inline skating, snowboarding, skiing, skateboarding, surfing

**Collecting:** stamps, coins, dolls, rocks, shells, miniatures, trading cards, cars, comics, action or animal figures, key chains, books, model trains or airplanes

**Nature exploration:** hiking, orienteering, bird watching, gardening, snorkeling, animal care, camping, astronomy, photography

**Intellectual exploration:** reading, computers, building models, foreign languages, astronomy, crossword puzzles, trivia, chess, historical reenactment, video games, board games

**Home arts:** pottery or clay, crafts, sewing, knitting, quilting, embroidery, weaving, cooking, scrapbooks, basket making, baking

Note that some hobbies fit in more than one category. Horseback riding, for example, is a way to explore nature or to compete with other riders. Rock collecting can involve outdoor hiking, studying the origin of different specimens, and coming up with a creative way to display your treasures. Hobbies can be as unique and diverse as the people who do them!

## Volunteer to Make a Difference

Another great way to push yourself in new directions is through volunteer work. Volunteering your time and energy can help you build skills while making a meaningful contribution to the world.

You may already be active in your community, pitching in for a worthy cause. Or maybe you volunteer through your religious organization or youth group. Some schools require students to perform a number of hours of community service. If you haven't been involved in any type of service project, you may wonder if your busy life is too full to fit in one more activity. Before you decide not to volunteer, consider the benefits of taking the time to do for others.

Being of service can give you a chance to give back—to make the place where you live better by cleaning up a park, painting a mural over a graffiti-filled wall, or starting a community vegetable garden in a vacant lot. Volunteering can provide you with an opportunity to connect with others—senior citizens at a nursing home, adults or kids in a shelter, or new people who have moved to your community. And volunteering can offer a way to let your voice be heard—writing letters about a cause you believe in or joining an organization that shares your ideas and values.

Tweens and teens who volunteer gain new experiences and broader views about life—they expand their vision of the world. When your vision of the world grows, so does your vision of yourself. Volunteering means accomplishing—and whenever you accomplish something, you feel better about who you are.

**CHECK IT OUT**

**Do Something**
**www.dosomething.com**
This organization connects volunteers with service opportunities. Visit the website to learn how you can get involved in your community.

**Serve.gov**
**www.serve.gov**
Find service ideas, tools for completing projects, and opportunities to share your experiences with others at this site.

# Make the Most of Your Time

You only have twenty-four hours each day to do all the things you want to accomplish, and sleeping is going to take a large chunk of that time. Getting older means having a lot more to do—and less time to do it in! You have homework, activities, family responsibilities, and friendships to handle. Maybe it seems like the hours zip past, and you still have lots to do. Maybe you feel that you need more time for yourself.

Making decisions about how you spend your time takes a little practice, but it's worth it. Often, people don't realize how much time they spend on stuff that isn't that important. What usually happens is that they run out of time for activities that are important or more enjoyable. Activities that can eat up a lot of time include watching television, texting, playing video games, and being online—if you spend hours doing them.

This doesn't mean you have to spend every waking moment doing something productive! Sometimes you need time to unwind. You can daydream, doodle, hang out in your room, or lie back and watch the clouds drift by. These activities give your brain and body a chance to rest and gather the energy you'll need for more active pursuits.

 **Tracking Your Time**

To find out if you're making the most of your time, keep track of what you do for one week and how much time each activity takes. (Focus mainly on your time before and after school.) Record the time you spend on activities like sports, music, or clubs, as well as time spent with family and friends. Make a note of what you do during your alone time, too.

After one week, review your list of activities. Put a ☺ next to the ones you enjoyed and a ☹ next to the ones you didn't. Put a ✓ next to the activities you had to do. Place an X by any nonessential activities you could have left out or shortened. Then draw a ★ next to the activities you wish you could have spent more time on.

Now study your list. Are there a lot of frowns and Xs? Maybe you can find ways to cut out activities you don't like or cut down on time-wasters.

Maybe you have a lot of stars on your list? If so, can you find more time to do these activities you enjoy? Do you have lots of checkmarks? This could mean you have too many responsibilities right now and not enough time to be with friends or by yourself. Is there an activity you're willing to give up to make time for other things? Ask a friend or an adult to look at your list and give you some suggestions.

One way to make the most of the time you have is to create to-do lists each day or week. These lists help you see everything you need to accomplish. Start by making a list of all your tasks and responsibilities, and then rank them in order of importance. Those are the things you must do first. Will some of your high-priority tasks take a lot of time? Break them down into shorter assignments and put those in order of importance. Cross off each job you complete. If you want, make a new list of the things you still have left to do.

Many people use calendars or day planners, as well as to-do lists. These tools, which you can find online, allow you to see your days, weeks, and months at a glance. You can keep a record of appointments, scheduled events, and other important activities. You'll probably find that keeping track encourages you to better plan your days and stay focused on meaningful activities.

# Set Goals to Beat the Procrastination Blues

What if certain tasks just aren't getting done? Maybe you keep shuffling them to new days on your calendar or transferring them from one to-do list to the next—also known as procrastinating. Procrastination is putting off and putting off and putting off what you need to do, until the very last moment. Then you reach a point where you feel totally stressed out because the deadline is approaching and you haven't made any progress. You end up rushing around, feeling frustrated and upset, and not doing a very good job.

A lot of people have a problem with procrastination, including adults. Few people look forward to doing things that aren't much fun or that seem difficult. Waiting until the last minute is a way to get out of the job—until the last minute arrives, the big job isn't done, and time has almost run out. Other people put off doing things because they expect perfection of themselves. They feel so much pressure to be "the best" and to do a "perfect" job that they're overwhelmed before they even get started.

Goal setting is a skill that can help you beat the procrastination blues. The key here is to set realistic goals—ones you have a good chance of reaching. You can set a goal to become more physically fit, for example, or to save more money. Or you can aim to make some new friends or to complete a school project on time.

# TRY IT   Setting Goals

Goal setting isn't a difficult skill, but it takes practice. How do you start? First, decide on a goal that has meaning to you. Goals can be long-range or short-range. Long-range goals are ones you want to reach in the future—six months or a year from now, for example. Short-range goals are more immediate—ones you hope to achieve in a matter of days or weeks. Start by thinking long-range. What do you really want? Higher grades on your report card is a worthy long-range goal, for example, and one that will take time to accomplish.

Now think of some manageable short-range goals that can help you reach the big goal. Maybe you'd like to do well on your next math test or turn in your social studies homework on time this week. List the steps you'll need to take to accomplish these short-range goals. When do you need to take each one? Set a target date. Keep track of your progress on your goals by recording them on the computer or in a notebook. List long- and short-term goals along with the dates by which you want to complete them. You might also include on this document ideas for staying on track, potential problems (along with solutions), and people who can help you reach goals.

# Goal-Setting Sheet

**Long-range goal:**

Target date for reaching it:

**Three short-term goals to help me get there:**

**Short-term goal #1:**

Target date:

**Short-term goal #2:**

Target date:

**Short-term goal #3:**

Target date:

Ideas for staying on track with my goals:

Potential problems:

How to deal with them:

People who can help me:

Goals are something you do for you. It's a waste of your time and energy to go for a goal you don't believe in or want for yourself (for instance, a goal that's important to your mom or dad but doesn't hold much meaning for you). When setting your long-range and short-range goals, ask yourself why you value these accomplishments. Are they truly meaningful to you? Will they make you feel good about yourself and the person you're becoming? If so, then go for it!

# Take Care of Your Money

You can use your decision-making skills to manage your money, too. Do you already earn your own money or get an allowance from your parents? If so, where do you fit on the money spectrum: a spender, a saver, or somewhere in-between? Some people have a hard time handling money; it always seems to disappear from their grasp. Others know how to hold on to what they have and keep making more. But most people probably fall somewhere in the middle; they spend money on things they really want and try to save a little for the future—but they don't have a clear idea of what their budget is.

Many tweens and teens learn their money habits from their families. Families have different approaches to money—and different rules about it, too. Parents, for example, differ on allowances. In some families, the allowance is based on the number of chores that are done. In others, the allowance is given freely whether or not work is done around the home. And in still other families, an allowance may be fixed with extra chores earning extra money. Some families don't have money to give as an allowance. And some parents simply don't believe in giving an allowance.

If you earn an allowance, chances are you're wishing for more than you get. Do you feel you deserve to have your allowance raised? Maybe it's time to talk to your parents about your expenses. Do you need more money for school supplies, clothes, or materials for your hobby?

Think about how to approach your parents about this issue. Don't pick a time when they seem grumpy or rushed, or when money is especially tight at home. When the time is right, you could start the conversation by telling them some good reasons for giving you a raise. Have you been doing more chores? Buying more basics for yourself (clothes, shampoo, notebooks)? Need cell phone minutes? Saving for a big purchase? Give your parents a chance to share their point of view, too. There may be many reasons why they can't raise your allowance—or pay you anything at all. If this is the case, you need to think about earning some extra cash on your own.

You may still be too young for a job with an outside company, but that doesn't mean you can't find other work. If your family has its own business, for example, you may be able to earn extra money by pitching in there. Or your family may know people who are willing to pay for chores like raking, mowing lawns, cleaning homes, walking dogs, babysitting, gardening, or shoveling snow. You can also take classes to learn skills that prepare you for different jobs. Many areas have programs for tweens and teens looking to work as babysitters, junior lifeguards, or other positions. Check with area schools and community agencies for opportunities.

If you have a skill or talent, you may be able to turn it into cash. Adults who need help with computers are a good source of income, for example. Are you good at Web design? Can you diagnose computer problems accurately? Are you handy with a screwdriver and other tools? Start a business that helps people put together furniture and other unassembled products. Good at sewing? Offer to hem clothing or repair split seams. Do you have a talent for crafts? Create and sell jewelry, picture frames, scrapbooks, T-shirts, greeting cards, or other items.

As a one-time money-raising event, you could hold a tag sale. Start with the items you no longer want, and then offer to clean out the garage

> "I've had a job after school for six months. I spend some of my money on clothes and other stuff, but most I save for college."
> **—Henri, 14**

 **Making a Budget**

A budget helps you keep track of how you spend and save. When you budget your money, you record your earnings, expenses (the money you spend), and savings (the money you have left after paying your expenses). On the computer or a sheet of paper, track your expenses month by month. You might set up six columns that look something like this:

|  | Week 1 | Week 2 | Week 3 | Week 4 | Totals |
|---|---|---|---|---|---|
| **Earnings** |  |  |  |  |  |
| **Fixed expenses** |  |  |  |  |  |
| **Flexible expenses** |  |  |  |  |  |
| **Savings** |  |  |  |  |  |

Earnings are the money you make. Expenses can fall into two categories: (1) fixed expenses, which don't change, and (2) flexible expenses, which do change. Fixed expenses might include the amount you need for buying your lunch at school or what you spend on materials for your business. Flexible expenses might include entertainment like movies, magazines, online charges, or gifts for your friends. You can spend less on your flexible expenses if you want to have more money to save.

and closets, and with your family's permission, sell the items they no longer want. If you decide to sell online, get an adult to help you sell your stuff. You can invite friends to bring items to sell and help you on the day of the sale. Other ideas include holding a bake sale or creating a talent show and charging admission, if you know others who are interested in participating (of course, you'll have to share the profits). Make sure you post plenty of signs to advertise your special event, and then take them down afterward.

You can keep your savings in a sock under your bed or stuffed in a drawer, but a smarter place would be in a savings account at the bank. You might also save your earnings in a money market account or CD (certificate of deposit), both of which you can learn about at a bank. All of these accounts allow you to earn interest, or an amount the bank gives you for use of the money you've deposited. Another option is to invest your savings in shares of stock. That means you own a small percentage of a company of your choice. Or you can look into mutual funds, which let you invest small amounts of money in a large number of companies. It's important to discuss these different options with an adult at home before moving forward.

**CHECK IT OUT**

*The Kid's Guide to Money: Earning It, Saving It, Spending It, Growing It, Sharing It* by Steven Otfinoski. This book has information on getting a job, starting a business, and being smart with the money you earn.

**Money Talks**
**moneytalks4teens.ucdavis.edu**
Visit this site for information on spending money wisely, growing savings, and setting up a bank account.

# Get Ready for What's Next

Soon you'll be in high school and considering college, a trade school, the military, or a career. While those days may seem far, far in the future, they're actually not. You probably thought middle school was a long way off when you were a little kid—but look how quickly you got here!

Do you ever daydream about your future? What are these dreams like? Do they include an exciting career, a romantic relationship, travels to amazing places, possibly some (terrific) kids and a nice home? Do daydreams have to be realistic? Not at all. Maybe you imagine exploring Mars or climbing Mount Everest. Whatever your dreams are, they're telling you something about yourself. And they're offering you a safe way to explore careers, lifestyles, and desires for your future. As you try each one on for size, you get a chance to see if it fits—and if it doesn't, you can begin a new dream, one that's more suited to you.

Daydreams help you:

- use your imagination
- build self-confidence
- realize that you can be a pilot, doctor, teacher, or an architect (anything you want!)
- picture yourself going anywhere or trying anything
- think about life as a spouse or parent
- prepare for your future

You may already know that dreaming only gets you so far. You also have to take action to make things happen in your life. Go for your goals, explore potential careers or educational opportunities, seek out role models and mentors, and keep believing in yourself.

## Role Models and Mentors

One way you can work toward your dreams is by finding role models and mentors. A role model is someone you admire so much that you try to use that person's life as a pattern for your own. Good role models encourage you to aim higher and be the best you can possibly be.

A mentor is someone who's available to help and advise you—in a hobby, a potential career, school, volunteer work, or any other aspect of your life. A role model and a mentor can be the same person (but don't have to be).

Do you have a role model? You don't have to know him or her personally. Many people use

"There's a woman in my neighborhood who owns two food shops. She's always nice to the customers who come in. I think I'd like to own a business one day."

**—Raina, 12**

sports figures or famous heroes as their role models. Look for who has overcome disadvantages or tough times and ended up successful. And remember that success isn't necessarily about being rich, famous, or powerful. Success can mean helping others, being generous, or acting with courage.

If you want to have a role model you can talk to, look for someone you know who has created the kind of life you'd like to lead yourself. Your role model can be a teen or an adult. Maybe the person is a great parent, donates time to the community, or is a talented achiever in a field of work you're interested in. Can you think of anyone right now who might make a good role model for you? If you need ideas, talk to a friend, parent, or teacher.

What happens if a role model you've chosen lets you down? Maybe you always looked up to a certain sports star—someone who gave you the courage to try out for a team and work hard in athletics. Now you've just heard this same star has been arrested for using drugs. How do you feel? Betrayed? Angry? Shocked? You've just learned that someone you thought could do no wrong made a mistake—a serious one. Will that role model continue to be one for you? It depends on what he or she does next.

Your role model might admit the mistake, apologize, and change his or her life for the better. In fact, that person may become even more of a role model, making better decisions in the future and helping others do the same. Or maybe the person continues making poor decisions, each one followed by an excuse or a refusal to admit any guilt. Role models are human, not superhuman, and like the rest of us, they make mistakes. You can still learn from these people, even if you don't look up to them like you did before. And you can take satisfaction in knowing that the person helped you, in some way, to make positive changes in your own life. Then you can look for a new role model to admire.

What about mentors? A mentor is a person older than you who can act as your guide and advisor. Many adults who enter the business world find a mentor who can help them achieve success in their careers. You can look for a mentor to help you navigate the middle school and high school years. A mentor might be a member of your family or a neighbor, teacher, coach, Girl Scout or Boy Scout leader, religious advisor, youth group leader, member of your community, or an older brother or sister of a close friend. An organization like Big Brothers Big Sisters of America may be able to set you up with a mentor as well.

Research shows that people who have mentors find it easier to make healthy decisions and positive choices in their lives. Having at least one adult to confide in—someone who has experienced the challenges of growing up and making decisions—can help you stand up for yourself and stand strong against negative peer pressure. If you know your mentor is in your corner, cheering you on in your efforts, you gain added confidence as you take charge of your life.

**Big Brothers Big Sisters of America**
**www.bbbs.org**
This organization connects tweens with responsible adults who can help explore interests or just be there to talk.

**Mentor**
**www.mentoring.org**
Visit this site to find community mentors. A search feature allows you to enter your zip code to find programs in your area.

## A Closing Thought . . .

What are the challenges and opportunities that lie ahead for you? You may be very sure that certain things will happen in your life (and some of them will). You'll probably also be surprised at how often you change your mind or your direction over the years. Middle school is full of surprises. You'll find that situations—good and bad—will come up unexpectedly and may cause you to adjust where you're going. When that happens, use the Survival Tips you've learned in this book. They can help you keep moving forward!

"I thought that when I got to middle school I'd automatically be treated like an adult and know what to do. But it doesn't happen that way. You don't have all the answers just because you're a little older. I guess there are a lot of things I still have to learn."
—**Liz**, 11

"I'm excited about not being a kid anymore. Being a teenager will be fun. Learning to drive, earning money, thinking about college, and being more independent. Every day I am getting closer to all those things."
—**Kendra**, 13

"I just finished middle school. I'm curious about what's going to happen to me in high school. I know I'll have more freedom, but who knows what else is out there for me? I guess I'll eventually find out!"
—**Randall**, 14

# Index

## A

Above the Influence (website), 103, 147

Acne, 3, 23–24

Activities
extracurricular, 137–139
family, 82–83
hobbies, 150–153
volunteering, 82, 153–155

ADHD/ADD, 122–123

Adrenaline, 50, 149

Advertising aimed at teens, 42–43, 147

Aggressiveness, compared to assertiveness, 101

Alcohol use, 100, 146–147

Allowances, 160–161

American Academy of Dermatology (website), 23

American Cancer Society, 24

Anger
management, 59–60
school violence, 106–107

Anorexia, 16, 18

Antiperspirants, 22

Appearance
braces, 35–36
clothes and fashion, 40–43
feelings about, 26, 43
glasses, 37
hair removal, 38–40
piercing, 38
self-image, 33–35

Artistic expression, 152, 153

Assertiveness
compared to aggressiveness, 101
dealing with bullying, 103–106
helpful tips, 100–101
self-esteem and, 29

Athletes
appearance of, 41
as role models, 165–166

Athlete's foot, 22

Athletics, *See* Sports

Author contact information, 5

## B

*Be Confident in Who You Are* (Fox), 30

Betrayal by friends, 92–93

Big Brothers Big Sisters of America (website), 167

B.J. Pinchbeck's Homework Helper (website), 124

Body changes
awkward stage, 35
in boys, 2–3, 8–9
coping with, 12–13
feelings about, 12–13, 25, 35
in girls, 2–3, 9–11

Body image, *See* Appearance

Body language, 67

Body odor, 21–22

Body piercing, 38

Boys
body changes, 8–9
erections and ejaculation, 8
facial hair, 8
shaving, 38–40
voice changes, 8

# G

# H

# About the Authors

**Harriet S. Mosatche, Ph.D.,** is an award-winning author of several books, including three she coauthored with her daughter. Harriet has been a tenured college professor, psychology department chair, and Girl Scouts of the USA vice-president. Currently president of The Mosatche Group (mosatchegroup.com), Harriet provides program development, training, grant-writing, and evaluation support to schools, community groups, and national organizations. She also serves on the American Bar Association Advisory Committee to the Commission for Youth at Risk and the Advisory Boards of both New Moon Media and Heartland Truly Moving Pictures.

Harriet often appears on television, radio, and the Internet; in books, magazines, and newspapers; and at conferences, providing expert advice. As online advice columnist "Dr. M," she responds to questions from tweens, teens, young adults, and parents at AskDrM.org.

**Karen Unger, M.A.,** is an award-winning writer and editor and works at a college of the liberal arts and sciences. As manager of program development at Girl Scouts of the USA, she directed projects and developed many resources for girls and women. She has also taught English as a second language as a college instructor and worked as a senior editor for a children's book publisher.

In addition to *Too Old for This, Too Young for That!,* Karen is the coauthor of *Where Should I Sit at Lunch? The Ultimate 24/7 Guide to Surviving the High School Years.* She has also published stories based on her experience as a Peace Corps volunteer in Liberia, West Africa. When she isn't busy writing, Karen enjoys spending time with her husband and son.

# Other Great Books from Free Spirit

## Be Fit, Be Strong, Be You
*by Rebecca Kajander, C.P.N.P., M.P.H., and Timothy Culbert, M.D.*

Whether they are underweight, overweight, or just the right weight, this book shows kids how to take a positive, holistic approach to their health and be the boss of their own wellness. Specific tips on eating, exercise, and self-esteem include planning meals and healthy "grabbable snacks," food journaling, getting daily exercise, using affirmations, and practicing complementary healthcare skills such as positive imagery and yoga. For ages 8 & up

*96 pp., color illust., softcover, 6" x 8"*

## No B.O.!
### The Head-to-Toe Book of Hygiene for Preteens
*by Marguerite Crump, M.A., M.Ed.*

Who needs acne? Stinky feet? B.O.? Good hygiene can make a big difference in how kids feel about themselves during puberty, as well as how others feel about them. This frank, reassuring, humorous book covers the physical changes boys and girls experience and offers tips on caring for oneself from head to toe. Fascinating facts, friendly suggestions, and funny illustrations combine for "tween-appeal." For ages 9–13.

*128 pp., 2-color, illust., softcover, 7" x 9"*

## Your Life in Comics
### 100 Things for Guys to Write and Draw
*by Bill Zimmerman*

What's more fun for tween guys than reading comics? Making their own. *Your Life in Comics* lets boys ages 9–13 do just that. Rather than provide the story, this interactive book for guys allows them to decide what happens by using words and drawings of their creation. For ages 9–13.

*128 pp., 2-color, illust., softcover, 6" x 9"*

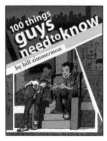

## 100 Things Guys Need to Know
*by Bill Zimmerman*

Advice for guys on all kinds of issues, including fitting in, bullies, school, peer pressure, and more. Graphic-novel-style illustrations, quotes from boys, survey results, facts, and stories make this an entertaining read. For ages 9–13.

*128 pp., 2-color, illust., softcover, 8" x 10½"*

## Speak Up and Get Along!
Learn the Mighty Might, Thought Chop, and More Tools to Make Friends, Stop Teasing, and Feel Good About Yourself
*by Scott Cooper*

A handy toolbox of ways to get along with others, this book presents 21 strategies kids can learn and use to express themselves, build relationships, end arguments and fights, halt bullying, and beat unhappy feelings. Includes a note to adults. For ages 8–12.
*128 pp., 2-color, illust., softcover, 6" x 9"*

## Stick Up for Yourself!
Every Kid's Guide to Personal Power and Positive Self-Esteem (Revised and Updated Edition)
*by Gershen Kaufman, Ph.D., Lev Raphael, Ph.D., and Pamela Espeland*

Simple words and real-life examples teach assertiveness, responsibility, relationship skills, choice making, problem solving, goal setting, anger management, and more. For ages 8–12.
*128 pp., illust., softcover, 6" x 9"*

## What to Do When You're Scared & Worried
*by James J. Crist, Ph.D.*

From a dread of spiders to panic attacks, kids have worries and fears, just like adults. This is a book kids can turn to when they need advice, reassurance, and ideas. For ages 9–13.
*128 pp., 2-color, illust., softcover, 5³/₈" x 8³/₈"*

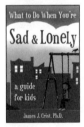

## What to Do When You're Sad & Lonely
*by James J. Crist, Ph.D.*

All kids feel sad and lonely sometimes. Growing numbers of children are living with depression, a disease often mistaken for sadness. This reassuring book offers strategies and tips kids can use to beat the blues and blahs, get a handle on their feelings, make and keep friends, and enjoy their time alone. For ages 9–13.
*128 pp., 2-color, illust., softcover, 5³/₈" x 8³/₈"*

## Middle School Confidential™ Series
*by Annie Fox, M.Ed.*

Middle school can be complicated—added classroom responsibilities, changing family dynamics, fitting into a shifting social scene. . . . This series features a blend of fiction and practical advice for these issues. Books include *Be Confident in Who You Are, Real Friends vs. the Other Kind,* and *What's Up with My Family?* For ages 11–14.
*Each book: 96 pp., color, illust, softcover, 6" x 8"*

# Free Spirit's
# Laugh & Learn™ Series

Solid information, a kid-centric point of view, and a sense of humor combine to make each book in our Laugh & Learn series an invaluable tool for getting through life's rough spots. For ages 8–13. *72–128 pp., illust., softcover, 5¹/₈" x 7"*

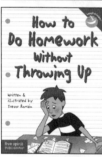

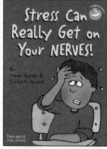

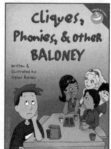

**Interested in purchasing multiple quantities?**
Contact edsales@freespirit.com or call 1.800.735.7323 and ask for Education Sales.

**Many Free Spirit authors are available for speaking engagements, workshops, and keynotes.** Contact speakers@freespirit.com or call 1.800.735.7323.

*For pricing information, to place an order, or to request a free catalog, contact:*

**Free Spirit Publishing Inc.**
**toll-free 800.735.7323 • help4kids@freespirit.com • www.freespirit.com**